STILLWATER STRONG
Loyal and True

by D. Scott Petty

Foreword by Mike Gundy

Cover Design: Mike Staubus, Eskimo Joe's

Editor: Kristine Waits

Assistant Editor: Quinn Baldwin

Book Layout & Design: Stephanie Greenlee, Beacon Public Relations

Photography Credit: David Bitton – Stillwater NewsPress, Michelle Charles – Stillwater NewsPress, CNN, Jeannie Dibble, Rhoda Hughes, Gary Lawson, Edmon Low Library, KFOR – NBC Affiliate, KOCO – ABC Affiliate, Oklahoma City, Niki Mittasch, Oklahoma State University, Leo and Sharon Schmitz, Niki Strauch, Stillwater Strong, Adam and Sara Wyatt

Reviewers: Crystal Byers, Hal Ellis, JD, Liz Lee, Mayor Gina Noble, Catherine Petty, Gerri Petty, Denise Webber

Book profits will support the construction of the Stillwater Strong Memorial. Upon funding completion of the Memorial, future book profits will continue supporting underfunded priorities for Stillwater Medical and the Stillwater community.

For more information, visit: www.stillwaterstrong.org

STILLWATER STRONG
Loyal and True

by D. Scott Petty

Foreword by Mike Gundy

*This book is dedicated to every law enforcement officer,
first responder, physician, nurse, volunteer, student, and citizen
who has ever responded to the trauma and recovery
of an unexpected tragic event.*

FOREWORD

When Scott Petty told me he was writing a book about the events relating to the 2015 OSU Homecoming tragedy, he explained to me that he wanted to share a collection of witness, victims, and first responder perspectives to reflect Stillwater's and Oklahoma State's inspirational stories of recovery and healing. I knew I would not only want to read a book like that, but also to help propel its purpose because I remember the day well.

The text messages came flooding in and it was apparent something was wrong. These weren't the normal well-wishes that we commonly receive the morning of a game.

"Are you okay?"

"Please let me know you're safe."

"Did you hear what happened at the Homecoming parade?"

This was the general tone of the messages we were getting. And when I say "we" in this case, I mean people throughout the Stillwater and Oklahoma State community.

You see, this was bigger than football. This touched all of us.

As the morning progressed and more information rolled in, we heard stories of people being hospitalized with serious injuries and even worse. It was bad.

We at Oklahoma State have experienced real tragedies before, but more on that later. For now, I'll just say that familiar sinking feeling was reignited inside of many of us on the morning of October 24, 2015.

For me personally, the first question upon hearing news of the crash was clear – is my family okay? My oldest son Gavin was away at school in Arkansas, but my other two sons, Gunnar and Gage, could have easily been on the scene with friends. Once I confirmed that everyone was okay, my focus immediately shifted to our players and their families and friends who were in town for the game. We have a roster of about 125 and they reported no injuries.

Relief.

But don't confuse relief with normalcy. As would be expected, all of us were wanting to know more about what happened and who was involved. Our families were confirmed to be unharmed, but we all had friends, classmates and others who we care about that we didn't have confirmation on. There were more questions than answers at that point of the morning, and they were serious questions.

We were in a state of uncertainty and dreading what we didn't know, but the fact remained that our team had a football game against Kansas at 2:30 p.m. that afternoon. There was some talk about whether the game would be cancelled or not, but that kind of decision is made above me. My job was to assume that we were going to play and to have the team mentally focused and prepared to play a football game just hours after innocent people lost their lives just a few blocks away from the stadium. You can see the issue that we faced, because whether we admitted it or not, we were all emotional and distracted about what happened at the corner of Hall of Fame and Main.

Word eventually came to us that the game would be played as scheduled, so we proceeded with our typical game day routine that we've had for years. Included in that routine is a team meeting right before we leave the Atherton Hotel to embark on "The Walk" to Boone Pickens Stadium. At that meeting, I addressed the group the best way I could think of – by telling them the truth. I told them that there are some things in our lives that we control and some things in our lives that we don't control. I told them that we needed to go out there and play the game, and when the game was finished, we needed to help the people and families who were affected by what happened earlier in the morning.

We left for The Walk, but it was understandably different that day. The sound of news helicopters was mixed into the sound of the band as it marched ahead of us. Keep in mind, The Walk happened just two hours after the crash, so everything was still raw and unknown. Even with that as the backdrop, some fans tried their best within reason to encourage our players as they approached the stadium.

When it was time for us to take the field for the game, we ran out of the tunnel and to our sideline like we always do, but this time, our players knelt on the green AstroTurf field to say the Lord's Prayer for everyone to see. As anyone who has ever been involved in our program would tell you, we have come together to say the Lord's Prayer regularly over the years, but that normally happens within the walls of our locker room and not in front of the public. But this was a time to do it for the victims.

While recognizing and acknowledging the tragedy of the morning and the profound impact that it had on the families involved, I also feel it's appropriate to recognize and acknowledge how proud I was of our players and of the Oklahoma State family that day. I believe God challenges people who can handle the challenges with strength, and this was the challenge He presented to us that day. Oklahoma State and its people responded with the same kind of steadfast resolve that we have every time we've faced circumstances like these.

I took particular pride in our players and am deeply appreciative of the maturity they showed, because it wasn't easy. Like I said earlier, we were all emotional, distracted and in search of answers. As coaches, we talk all the time to our players about handling adversity and controlling the things that you can control. We try to instill that into them, both as football players and as people, but this was a chance to see it come to light.

Despite the tragic event of the morning, the players were focused and sharp come game time. We won, 58-10. Maybe it's because they were mature enough to understand that they were playing for something bigger than themselves that day. After the game was over, we stuck to our regular post-game routine of talking to members of the media and that's where our players further displayed their maturity. Here are a couple of quotes from two of our team's leaders that day:

"I personally could see in guys' eyes, they wanted to get this done today and maybe give those people that had a complete shock, give them something to maybe brighten their day. Just to show that we're coming out today and we're doing it more than for just us, more than just our team. It's for everybody in this town and community and state."

– David Glidden

"I think that's a little bit of the point of the game today, we were able to, at least for ourselves and hopefully some other people, maybe shed some of that light. Just for a few hours. And I hope we did a good job of it."

– J.W. Walsh

A couple days later, our players were among a large group from Oklahoma State who loaded into buses and spread out among the area hospitals to visit some of the people who were injured at the parade. Hearing the victims' stories was remarkable, as there were stories of heroism within the crowd. I believe you'll enjoy reading more of these inspiring stories that Scott Petty has compiled of those who helped Before, During and After our 2015 Homecoming Tragedy.

–Mike Gundy, September 2017

STILLWATER STRONG

Loyal and True

by D. Scott Petty

Foreword by Mike Gundy

TABLE OF CONTENTS

INTRODUCTION

THE RIGHT THING

In 1993, I was in Chicago for a conference of the American Osteopathic Association (AOA), the medical association for osteopathic physicians. While in the Windy City, I attended a ceremony for the first African American President of the AOA, Dr. William G. Anderson, who had been involved in the civil rights movement in the 1960s. In a few short months, I would be picking him up at the Houston airport, so I wanted to meet him and introduce myself. Dr. Anderson would be providing an address to attendees at our Texas Osteopathic Medical Association annual conference.

A buzz began to spread throughout the convention hotel that two very well-known friends of Dr. Anderson's were standing next to him in the receiving line.

"Did you hear who's with him?" Someone said outside the convention hall. I wondered if it was perhaps Mohammad Ali or maybe Oprah Winfrey (I had heard she lived in Chicago). The prospect of meeting someone famous even for a minute was totally intriguing to me and my mind raced about whom it might be and what our brief exchange might be like. I felt like an aspiring musician meeting Elvis Presley.

I stood in a receiving line that wound its way up some stairs and down the long Great Hall. Guests and convention attendees — literally hundreds of us— moved just a few steps at a time, gradually inching our way to what was an impressive line of finely dressed people nodding and shaking hands, ending with Dr. and Mrs. Anderson. Standing close to them were their two long-time, good friends, one of whom I honestly don't recall hearing much about prior to the evening. His name was Andrew Young.

Mr. Young happened to be a former mayor of Atlanta, a well-known Civil Rights activist, a friend of Dr. Martin Luther King, Jr., a former United States Congressman, and had served as the Ambassador to the United Nations for President Jimmy Carter. However, at the time of our brief handshake, I knew none of that. My attention was transfixed on a woman standing approximately five feet tall. She was politely shaking hands with each person, and I could just barely see her from my distant position in line.

"Oh. My. Goodness." I thought to myself. "There stands an icon I've only read about in American History and have only seen on historic T.V. footage."

My mind began racing as we slowly shuffled closer. What meaningful exchange could I possibly have in only a five second hand-shake with a woman who had such an indelible fingerprint on American society? I knew I wanted to have a thoughtful interaction, but I'd be lucky if I got even a few seconds. As I finally approached her, I extended my right hand, which she engaged, and then I gently placed my left on top of hers leaning down.

"Ms. Parks, my name is Scott Petty. It is a great honor to meet you," I said. "I just want to sincerely say thanks for what you've done for all Americans." I thought to myself, "She must be really tired of standing here shaking all of these hands with people she'll never see again!"

Standing with a reserved, practically shy demeanor, the Mrs. Rosa Parks looked me in the eyes. About to speak to me was the woman who wouldn't relinquish her seat for a white man in the "colored section" on that Montgomery, Alabama city bus on December 1, 1955.

With more humility than I believe I have ever witnessed she said, "Thank you, sir. It's nice to meet you, too. You know, people just have to do the right thing." Her simple and sweet words have consistently nudged me for nearly 25 years.

"Yes ma'am, I agree. Thank you for joining us," I stammered. What?! Wait! I think I just told her thank you for joining us. I meant thank you for being here for Dr. Anderson.

Just six years out of college, this would be the first memorable occasion when I walked away from a powerful, potentially life-changing moment wishing I had been more eloquent and less dorky. At 27-years-old I was such a rookie, however Mrs. Parks herself could not have been more composed and genuine after she had already stood there for close to an hour shaking hands and greeting people from the medical profession.

She obviously felt it was important to honor Dr. Anderson as the first black president of the AOA. For me, her influence will last my lifetime.

My hope from our brief exchange, is that now this story, her words to me, and her life of example will last far beyond her actions and involvement in The Civil Rights Movement. "People just have to do the right thing," she had said. I replayed her statement in my mind. "People just have to do the right thing." I repeated it, thinking I never wanted to forget Mrs. Parks' plain-spoken words.

They were so few and simple, yet a most profound statement coming from this amazing woman.

"Do. The. Right. Thing." How many times did she repeat those uncomplicated words to her loved ones or to the Montgomery, Alabama law enforcement that December and in the days and years to come until her passing in 2005? How many people did she repeat those same simple words to over the nearly 50 years after the incident on the bus that became a national reminder of our unfairly segregated society in which she and other generations have grown up?

She was in the right place at the right time and what a difference she made, for being a human that had the determination and strength to "do the right thing." She was just one voice, but she found the strength to pursue a path most were not willing to take. Doing the right thing should help the greater good. It should drive home the ambition of making the big picture better, even if that means your personal priorities and interests are temporarily or permanently placed on the back-burner.

Having made mistakes in my life, I've reflected on her insightful words directed to me in that minimal interaction we had in Chicago. It was not just my parents and my in-laws, but Mrs. Parks, who inspired me to volunteer my time, to help others and try to take the high road.

I have thought about her statement often over the last 25 years since meeting her. I never anticipated her words might have the opportunity to help inspire a different kind of movement and healing assistance, when so many in our community and beyond were hurting both physically and emotionally from such a public trauma.

Through the years I have continued to think about Mrs. Parks and her unselfish, humble persona. In hindsight, I could have simply shaken her hand and said, "So nice to meet you," and just continued on into the celebratory evening. It was nice to meet her, and it would have been the honest truth, but maybe looking into my youthful eyes she detected a seed-planting opportunity.

I graduated from, worked for and love deeply, Oklahoma State University, and as the Executive Director of the Stillwater Medical Foundation, I embraced an opportunity to help these homecoming crash victims. This true account and series of stories might explain how countless others also were compelled to do the right thing.

Many were in the right place at the right time and they had the ability to make it meaningful. I trust this story will provide others hope and can be an inspiration for you or for someone else, to be a light of hope when others need it most.

THE FACTS

DATE:	October 24, 2015
TIME:	10:29:54 a.m. Stillwater 911 Dispatch receives first call
LOCATION:	Stillwater, Oklahoma,
	Intersection of Main Street and Hall of Fame Avenue
EVENT:	Oklahoma State University Homecoming, Sea of Orange Parade
HEADLINE:	Car Crash Kills Four Approximately Fifty Injured

Standing before media, microphones, and cameras, in front of the City Hall, Captain Kyle Gibbs of the Stillwater Police Department describes what unfolded at the Oklahoma State University Sea of Orange Homecoming Parade, creating a tragic end to a festive and historic OSU and Stillwater event.

"This morning near the conclusion of the OSU Homecoming Day Parade at Hall of Fame and Main, we had a traffic collision involving a single vehicle, which was a 2014 Hyundai Elantra driving south on Main Street. It first struck an unmanned police motorcycle which was working the parade assignment. It continued and struck a crowd of people and that occurred at approximately 10:30 a.m. At this time, we have three confirmed fatalities. Eight critically injured have been flown from the scene by air ambulance; we know of seven serious injuries and an additional seven walking wounded. All of those have been sent to Stillwater Medical Center for treatment.

The driver of the car was arrested for driving under the influence and that person was taken into custody at the scene. She is a 25-year-old Stillwater resident and she is currently in jail here at the police department.

At this point the police department's reconstruction team is on scene. We treat these like we would any homicide investigation. It will probably take several days to get information as to the cause of the accident, and we will update everyone as that information becomes available."

The public later learned that tests concluded the driver of the car was not under the influence of drugs or alcohol at the time of the crash. The driver intentionally drove her car into the crowd.

Aerial photo of Hall of Fame and Main Street before Hall of Fame Avenue extended east of Main Street to Perkins Road circa 1978. The photo reflects an intersection with no traffic signal and limited development.

Flashing back to that fateful Stillwater intersection 32 years earlier; if you were a college student like I was in 1983, and certainly before that time, Hall of Fame didn't stretch east beyond Main Street to Perkins Road. In fact, it stopped at Main Street, just across the street from where Hastings stood.

That building on the southwest corner of the intersection was previously a quaint Safeway grocery store that served our citizens for many years. This was before students and families renting VHS movies and video games made Hastings a true Stillwater entertainment mecca on the corner of one of our community's most prominent intersections. In fact, if one were to place a pin in the exact center of our city, more than likely this would be the intersection.

Directly across from the old Safeway turned Hastings, a field with waist high Johnson grass and a thick stand of trees stood concealing the old train tracks. Gazing east towards current day Food Pyramid (formerly Albertsons), there was a well-lit, legitimate Putt-Putt miniature golf course, the Starlight Drive-In theater, a Baskin Robbins Ice Cream shop, and a mobile home park situated in the distance.

Peering across that stand of trees and the deep field of Johnson grass was property owned by some budding entrepreneurs. Those visionaries speculated one day this area in the center of town could become thriving, bustling with business. Little did they know, this intersection would draw the nation's attention toward tragedy. And ultimately something bigger... hope.

BEFORE

─────────── ℰ ───────────

Building Strength

"Do something wonderful, people may imitate it."
Albert Schweitzer

STILLWATER

O ur small, eclectic city of Stillwater, Oklahoma, with approximately 50,000 residents has experienced gradual and positive economic growth since 1890, when our land grant school got its start. Stillwater's residents and Oklahoma State University alumni have called her home even before Oklahoma established statehood in 1907. They have come and they have gone. However, this town intertwines through the fabric of one's soul, so once you've lived here, you never truly leave.

Some return for the excitement of Division I athletic events, hoping to baptize their visiting children and grandchildren into her impassioned orange waters. Others relocate to run a business or simply retire and support their alma mater. Today, Stillwater is growing her medical, aerospace, and multiple technological industries into magnificent opportunities for others. With the proper economic influences, Stillwater could honestly become the heart of the 'Silicon Plains.'

Do Stillwater and Oklahoma State University still produce successful and inspirational entrepreneurs? You better believe it! Oklahoma State University graduates have gone on to become founders, CEOs, and leading executives in companies such as Pfizer Pharmaceuticals, Cerner Corporation, Fossil, Capitol Records Nashville, Arista Records Nashville, Warner Music Group, AT&T, Praxair, and Victoria's Secret.

Ed Roberts, a 1968 Oklahoma State University, Electrical Engineering graduate, is widely known as the father of the first personal computer. In fact, Ed hired a youthful Bill Gates and Paul Allen after they reached out to him seeing his Altair computer on the cover of Popular Electronics magazine in 1975. Ultimately becoming a rural internal medicine physician and farmer due to a no compete agreement, Dr. Roberts later started another software company.

Moreover, some of the highest leadership in entities such as MTV Networks, YouTube, BlackBerry, Claire's, Oakley, Ditch Witch, PING, ExxonMobil, ConocoPhillips, Coronet Flooring, ISN Software, Kicker Audio, and Far Niente wines have been OSU graduates. Heck, given the impact on our globe by some of these notable graduates, one would have to admit, even OSU Alumni like Stillwater born actor and model James Marsden, entertainer Garth Brooks, and Dick Tracy cartoon creator Chester Gould might have jaw dropping moments reflecting on our tremendous alumni in business and entertainment leadership roles.

As many good things have come out of Stillwater, this little city has had its share of tragedies.

AN EARLY TRAGIC AIRPLANE CRASH – 1951

As a land grant university, many in the state of Oklahoma know Oklahoma State University was founded on Christmas Day 1890, under the Morrill Act. Originally known as Oklahoma Agricultural and Mechanical College (Oklahoma A&M), President Henry G. Bennett began leading OAMC on July 1, 1928, after serving as the president at Southeastern State College in Durant, Oklahoma. Several years later, President Bennett outlined a bold plan defining needs for multiple new campus structures in Stillwater.

He envisioned needs for a new library, a new home economics building, a new power plant, and a chemistry building. In addition, Bennett proposed a new poultry facility, a new agricultural engineering building, and more land for dairy operations. Bennett's forward thinking and inspirational blueprint for growth, charted a path for academic expansion ultimately impacting generations of Cowboys.

Despite the Great Depression, Bennett managed to build the first major structures of his strategic vision which provided necessary expansion of the college, as well as jobs for those suffering from unemployment. He committed the campus to maintain our stately, modified Georgian architecture which has remained consistent even as we've grown a multitude of new, more modern, and highly technological buildings.

Sadly, on December 22, 1951, almost 61 years to the day after our college was founded, President Henry G. Bennett and his wife, Vera, were two of 22 people killed in a plane crash in Tehran, Iran, during a snowstorm. They had been traveling abroad as part of the Point Four Program and were returning to Stillwater. President Bennett had been a dynamic trailblazer at Oklahoma A&M thus garnering the respect of leaders both nationally and globally.

Though still president of A&M at the time of the deadly plane crash, Bennett was on a leave of absence serving as director of the Technical Cooperation Administration, a program for developing countries which had been announced just two years earlier by U.S. President Harry S. Truman in his inaugural address. Bennett was a thoughtful man that took his passion and vision well beyond our borders to make a difference.

This was Stillwater's first true public tragedy and, regrettably, not our last. In fact, the Bennett's plane crash was the first of five very public tragedies reinforcing the brevity of life for our University in the heartland.

COWBOY BASKETBALL TRAGEDY – 2001

In much more recent history, our Cowboy faithful vividly remember January 27, 2001, when a Beechcraft King Air was one of three aircraft shuttling our basketball players, coaches, radio broadcast team and athletic staff back from the Colorado game after playing in Boulder. According to the report from the National Transportation Safety Board, the King Air lost tower contact at approximately 23,200 feet. The plane was found scattered across a snow-covered field near Strasburg, Colorado. Two pilots and eight members of our Cowboy men's basketball program died in that crash just east of Denver, Colorado.

In a heartbeat, I lost a friend and neighbor, 31-year-old Will Hancock whose wife, Karen, just two months earlier, had Andie their first born. No longer would we have a curbside chat as they walked around our block. Now Will's youthful widow would raise their daughter alone. Gratefully, as the head coach of the OSU Women's Soccer program, she would derive courage and support from close friends and family dealing with the ugly grind of a public catastrophe no one could explain.

Our school lost Bill Teegins, an award winning, engaging television sports anchor and Cowboy Basketball and Football play-by-play broadcaster, who came into our living rooms nightly from News9. We tuned him in throughout the year broadcasting from the road, or from sporting events we couldn't make it to due to kids' soccer games or other obligations. Bill had a knack for remembering names, in fact, he remembered mine from the first time we met. Maybe because I told him I grew up seeing him on Amarillo, Texas, television before he moved to Oklahoma City, but he thoughtfully called, not just me, but many others by name, which just made you feel good.

Gone was Jared Weiberg, an acquaintance really, but the younger brother of my friend and former fellow OSU Foundation employee at the time, Chad Weiberg. Today, Chad is with athletics at Oklahoma State. As a member of the OSU Basketball program, his brother, Jared, had both played and served as one of the team managers under Coach Eddie Sutton. He also attended church with our family and possessed an authentic, beaming smile boasting his enthusiasm for life and all things Poke.

Pat Noyes, Director of Basketball Operations had an upbeat, friendly demeanor and positive aura which influenced the team, coaches and fans. I did not know Pat as well as the others, but I knew him well enough to feel the bite from the loss of his young life and the erasing effect it had on our OSU family. During his service, they played a voicemail he had left a friend the day of the crash, and his enthusiastic persona was momentarily relived.

I didn't personally know the six other men that died in the crash, however, their association with Oklahoma State and their names are forever etched into our hearts as part of that sad day. Cowboy Basketball players Nate Fleming and Dan Lawson, along with trainer Brian Luinstra, broadcast engineer Kendall Durfey, pilot Denver Mills and flying enthusiast, Bjorn Fahlstrom were all lost in the gut-wrenching crash. Our school and alumni have done an admirable job of annually honoring and remembering these ten men and their impact on Oklahoma State.

On January 28, 2001, the Sunday morning after this plane crash occurred, the sun wasn't quite up yet. Running on little sleep and broken-hearted, I eventually migrated to our living room couch. Our then 5-year-old daughter, Catherine, had seen the illumination of the television flickering from down the hallway of her bedroom. I'm sure she thought someone was up too early watching cartoons so she inquisitively strolled in to investigate. She toddled down the hallway and spotted me focused on the news story on the screen. With the volume barely audible, she quietly walked in front of me and slid down close beside me trying to snuggle as I was watching the news. The serious tone of the television anchor and my stoic facial expression quickly conveyed we weren't watching cartoons. I placed my right arm around her shoulder and pulled my first born closer.

Out of the corner of my eye, I could see our little Catherine looking directly at me and then back at the screen. Back and forth a couple of times she gazed at the TV and then back at me. She saw tears streaming down my face. I thought that she didn't understand any of it, but she knew.

She recognized the gravity of something deep unfolding, something serious and painful to me. Without words she gently put her little palm on my cheek and felt my tears, keeping it there as if to convey she cared and everything would be okay.

Her compassion and patience filled a small corner in the void of my heart, but it was still minutes before I could speak. I choked back tears and tried to be strong as I contemplated an explanation of this catastrophic event, suitable for a 5-year-old.

COWGIRL BASKETBALL TRAGEDY - 2011

Cowgirl Head Basketball Coach Kurt Budke's youngest son, Brett, and our daughter, Catherine, were in the same class when the Budkes moved to Stillwater. The first day I met Kurt and Shelley, we were in one of the modular classrooms at Sangre Ridge Elementary School for fourth grade orientation. Our kiddos progressed on through middle school, junior high, and graduated from Stillwater High School in the class of 2014.

The Budke's two other children, Sara and Alex, were already in college when the news broke that their father had died tragically in the 2011 crash. I came to know Kurt as a genuinely good guy. He was a passionate father who loved his family, his community, and his Cowgirls. He holds the distinction of being the youngest coach ever inducted into the National Junior College Basketball Association Hall of Fame and his loss sent a shockwave through every rank of coaching.

On Friday, November 18, 2011, ten months after we observed the ten-year anniversary of the men's basketball Colorado crash, another unexpected event rocked Stillwater. Beloved and successful Cowgirl basketball head coach, Kurt Budke, and his brilliant, 36-year-old assistant coach, Miranda Serna, were killed along with pilots Paula and Olin Branstetter when their small plane crashed in Perry County, Arkansas, east of Little Rock. The coaches were on a recruiting trip and had become accustomed to flying in small, privately owned aircraft to make quick trips to visit nearby players.

Suddenly, our university, alumni, and the community of Stillwater had to deal with a third airplane crash. A decade earlier family, friends and fans gathered in the OSU Athletic Center to honor those lost in the 2001 crash. Some of those same mourners and many new, somberly made their way into Gallagher-Iba Arena to pay their respects for this tragic loss of life. How could one school again bear the pain of public loss of life within the Oklahoma State Athletics family?

OSU's Head Football Coach Mike Gundy had to address the enormously shocking event with his football team in an Iowa hotel as he prepared their undefeated Cowboy Football team to play Iowa State University on the road. Mike lost a good friend in Kurt Budke, a peer head coach, and someone with whom Mike had much in common.

The Cowboy Football team lost the game against the Iowa State University Cyclones that next night. As it turned out, that would be the only loss the Pokes would have that season eliminating the opportunity to be National Champions. There was still much to play for as the Cowboys won the Fiesta Bowl. This win gave our fans something about which to feel encouraged after losing Kurt and Miranda. However, one lesson our school and alumni were once again reminded of was that precious life means much more than wins and losses.

COMING HOME – 1977

Thoughts of a "Homecoming" should bring anticipation and excitement. The idea of coming home engenders the fun of seeing those not seen in the recent past. The idea of sharing an embrace with friends after a long absence from a place one previously considered home is what makes "homecomings" truly special reunions. Whether it be our military returning after being consistently in harm's way around the world defending our freedoms, or throngs of college alumni returning to their school gathering to reflect and relive the "good ol days," homecomings are special to anyone and everyone involved.

In the fall of 1977, the Alpha Gamma Rho (AGR) fraternity at Oklahoma State University was about to be led through unspeakable challenges by 20-year-old Paul Schulte, a junior from Kingfisher, Oklahoma. Like all fraternity elected leadership, Paul was one of the visionaries entrusted by their membership to guide his fraternity with maturity and resolve in all fraternity, campus, and community dealings.

Being raised in rural Oklahoma, Paul understood the importance of thinking before one spoke and respecting the authority of experience. His maturity was likely another clear reason his peers chose him to serve as an executive officer in their fraternity. When Paul agreed to assume the responsibility, he could not have known he would be thrust into the unenviable position he would encounter only two months into the school year.

Annually, at Oklahoma State's homecoming, fraternity and sorority living groups collaborate to build elaborate house decorations and homecoming parade floats honoring their alumni and Greek history. This décor consists of creatively constructed designs, involving colorful tissue decorated chicken wire, and complex mechanically engineered scenes moving or interacting within the theme of homecoming. The fall of 1977 was no different for the AGR house.

Paul was in his room preparing to meet a friend from the Sigma Nu house for breakfast shortly after sunup on the morning of Friday, October 14th.

At approximately the same time, an Agricultural Economics senior and chaplain of the AGR fraternity, Dennis Slagell from Hydro, Oklahoma, didn't have class until 10 a.m. Likewise, sophomore Steve Pope from Loyal, Oklahoma, had been up most of the night working on their house decoration along with Homecoming Director, Kevin Wilson from Beaver, Oklahoma. Several of them spent most of the twilight hours working on the engineering functions of their homecoming structure ensuring it was perfect. However, with the OSU Homecoming Walk-Around scheduled only hours away, their day was booked solid preparing for alumni, friends, and family members coming to Stillwater for homecoming festivities.

Steve rounded up some of the skilled guys who had been a big help knowing Friday's sands through the hour glass were slipping quickly once the sun was up. Dennis slid on his sneakers before stepping outside to help his AGR brothers put the finishing touches on their homecoming house decoration. The word "decoration" is probably an understatement, as the colorfully massive, story-telling structure stretched across the fraternity's front yard practically the length of their entire house.

On this beautifully crisp morning, Dennis decided to put on a jacket. Stepping onto the grass, he and the others began assessing the multiple tasks ahead needing completion before they could finish their final project, the AGR homecoming parade float. Other members and pledges of the AGR fraternity were slowly gathering in the front yard.

The entire AGR membership along with the women of Kappa Alpha Theta sorority, selected as their homecoming partners, worked tirelessly on the finishing touches for their house decoration. As the sun inched slowly above the off-campus buildings on the east side of Washington Street, also known as "The Strip," the handful of men were nearing completion on their last responsibilities ensuring the mechanical elements were functioning properly.

"Alright guys, let's get this scaffolding positioned so we can finish this north end," one brother said as several other guys gathered around the metal rod scaffolding preparing to walk it closer to the area needing completion. Some of the guys were completely unaware, two innocuous actions earlier that morning may have saved their lives. One, they had on jean jackets or insulated shirts with long thick sleeves and two, they had on sneakers instead of cowboy boots.

With Merle George, Randy Logan, Kevin Wilson, Billy Morgan, on two sides, and Dennis, Steve, Ted Tracy, a student from Illinois, and Keith Kissee, originally from Missouri, on the other two sides, they all slid their arms underneath the scaffolding bar, cradling the four sections of the horizontal rod in the buckle of their elbows as the guys had done so many times. In unison, they counted out loud, "One...Two...Three..." lifting on all four sides they elevated the heavy iron structure slowly, walking it toward the next desired position in the front yard. Both Steve and Dennis' insulated jackets created an unintentional barrier, so their skin was untouched by the metal structure.

They were hanging the ornate tissue-pomped, chicken wire on one of the elevated parts of the house decoration. However, something happened before the scaffolding was set and in position.

Like lightening, Steve saw the flash of light. His eyes widened like saucers as the throbbing spark of light traveled down the metal rod scaffolding. A powerful, riveting pop jolted and rocked the scaffolding as a 72,000-volt electrical current instantly rendered several of the men helpless. Steve rolled away from the structure into the alley between the AGR and Sigma Nu fraternities.

"Ted, we've got to get away from that, move! Roll... roll... roll!" Steve yelled.

In shock, both Ted and Steve stumbled to their feet and ran to the back door of the fraternity. Once inside they could still hear that sickening noise – the burning hum and buzz associated with electricity pulsing nearby.

Chaos erupting in the AGR front yard, the constant shockwave of electricity from the power line violently pulsed, throwing some of the men clear of the now fiercely shaking and popping structure. Dennis, Steve, Ted, Keith, and Billy were all shocked, blown away from the scaffolding, or severely shaken. Unbelievably, the three others were killed instantly.

Collecting their senses, guys nearby knew they couldn't physically grab the others stuck to the scaffolding to pull them to safety. In a panic, lunging to de-anchor his friends from this horrifying and deadly scene, one of their brothers had to be restrained as he attempted to do something which likely would have ended his life.

Handy with a rope from ranching, Dennis thought if he could find one he could possibly lasso and pull the three men from their trapped situation. They were locked to the scaffolding, but if he had a rope the electrical charge wouldn't be conducted through it to him. But there was no rope.

A young patrolman in the Stillwater Police Department for just one year named Norman McNickle assigned to be with a rookie officer on his very first day on the force sped to the AGR fraternity house. They were the first officers from the SPD on the scene. The electrical current still convulsing the scaffolding structure had literally welded the iron framework to the power-line. Getting the power of this line shut off would take several more minutes, but the loss of life was evident before the officers exited their patrol unit.

McNickle immediately radioed the dispatcher requesting every available ambulance in town to the scene. He wasn't sure that would be enough since there were only three units in Stillwater at the time.

Though thrown from the scaffolding, guys wearing tennis shoes, long-sleeves, or work gloves were grounded or semi-protected from the merciless electrical charge. The shock and devastation crushed the school's spirited homecoming weekend as well as the depths of people's hearts across Oklahoma and beyond.

Just hours before the OSU Homecoming Walk Around event was to begin, lying dead in their own front yard were OSU students from three rural Oklahoma communities. Freshmen Merle George of Manchester, Randy Logan of Elk City, and senior Kevin Wilson of Beaver, all died while enjoying the fellowship and brotherhood that comes from being part of something bigger than themselves.

Independently in disbelief, those injured and uninjured began trying to make sense of what just happened.

As one of AGR fraternity's leaders, Paul Schulte took the initiative to ensure their house mom, Mom Dot, was quickly sheltered in a neighboring fraternity shielding her from the sad loss and the anticipated press. Upon Paul's return to the AGR front yard, first responders and university officials asked Paul to identify the bodies of his three fallen friends. This gruesome task was beyond anything he ever imagined he would be required to do in college much less life.

When Paul returned to his own room in the fraternity house, he found waiting for him OSU President, Dr. Larry Boger, Director of the Inter-Fraternity Council, Jim Jordan, Vice President of Student Services, Norman Moore, and his fraternity advisor, Agricultural Economics professor, Dr. John Goodwin. Each of the men modeled compassion and courage.

An untold emotional and physical shock forever changed the hearts and minds of the 80 men living in the AGR fraternity house that fall. In reality, the entire University experienced a level of love and support they could not have anticipated.

Billy Morgan of Waukita, Oklahoma, was one of the critically injured victims. While Paul was visiting him at Stillwater Medical Center, they made the decision to completely remove the AGR/KAT homecoming decoration from the AGR front yard.

Steve Pope's dad, Bill, had been a freshman at Oklahoma A&M when school President Henry Bennett and his wife, Vera, died in the 1951 airplane crash in Iran. In a day of no cell phones and only land telephone lines, when Steve finally reached his mom and dad to tell them what had happened, Bill sensed the magnitude of his son's pain. He recalled the sadness of unexpectedly losing President Bennett. Now they had a tragic thread weaving a story of youthful life and sudden death, forever changing them in a spiritually bonding way.

Steve drove home to tiny Loyal, Oklahoma, that afternoon. Following a much-needed nap in the family's living room recliner, he went outside and walked dazed through his cattle. Steve was still reeling from the graphic loss of young life before his own eyes. Reconnecting with what he grew up loving, he found a defining level of consciousness. The familiarity of that field created a stabilization he never expected. He understood it. Spending quiet time with his livestock in the field next to the family home was the first minimal step toward grasping the brittleness of life at 19-years-old.

Steve's dad thoughtfully reflected with his son about how President Bennett's death devastated the campus. Bennett was a fantastic ambassador for Oklahoma and for the United States. As a former agricultural education teacher turned farmer and rancher, Bill reminded his son of life's fragileness and inspired him to take one day at a time and live life to the fullest.

With the anticipation of thousands of people pouring into the streets in just a few hours to observe the creative house decorations on which the fraternities and sororities had collaborated, a thoughtful group of members from Farmhouse and other fraternities arrived to dismantle the nearly completed but now sadly tarnished AGR house decoration. They could not remove the physical scars to the AGR property, nor could they remove the emotional ones.

According to Paul Schulte, Rev. John Roscoe from the Wesley Methodist Student Center across the street, Father Bob Schlitt of St. John's Catholic Church, and Rev. Charlie Baker from University Heights Baptist Church provided significant support and counsel to those needing to talk through the tragic scene and raw reality impacting the entire fraternity and campus family.

Key University leadership debated over whether or not to hold the homecoming parade the next morning. There was even discussion whether or not the OSU vs. Kansas State Football game should be played. However, the parade would go on, and the game would be played.

Before either of those events began, at 7:30 a.m. the next day, sincerely positioned behind a podium and before a standing-room-only crowd of over 1,000 mourners in the Seretean Center Concert Hall, Paul did his best to eulogize those three men. Inspired by their short lives and their homecoming passion, he encouraged attendees to make the most of the day reaffirming the important tradition started by those who came before them.

Having been propped up by the counsel of Rev. Baker, Paul attempted to infuse the meaning of brotherhood as well as the love he and his fraternity family felt. To the best of his ability, he highlighted the finest qualities each of these three college students possessed. He expressed gratitude for the heartfelt outpouring of love and compassion he, his brothers, and their families felt in the hours following the tragedy.

Upon conclusion of the somber and packed memorial service, the crowd emerged from the Seretean Center, slowly heading to "The Strip" where the parade was set to begin. Alumni and friends had already begun gathering along the parade route in anticipation of the strong support needed by the AGR fraternity and their families.

In the front yard of their fraternity house, stood Dr. Goodwin, Paul, Mom Dot, and most of the AGR fraternity membership. In a painful reverent manner, they watched the parade procession pass their fraternity.

As in every OSU Homecoming Parade since 1930, bands marched playing fight songs and energized music. Colorfully decorated floats rolled through the route but on this day, to the AGRs, it seemed more like a funeral procession rolling down Washington Street.

None of the AGRs expected to see their previously unfinished AGR/KAT homecoming float gliding down the street on The Strip. Compassionate OSU family members and their Greek brethren had banded arm-in-arm offering collective support for the AGR membership wrought with loss. Through Paul's clouded thoughts he could only think of Merle, Randy, Kevin, and their families. Why them? Why our fraternity? Why now?

As the float passed by the membership gazing in awe of this unexpected moment, they noticed a wreath adorning the back of the float, honoring the memory of those three boys with a large wreath ruminating; "In Memory of Merle George, Randy Logan, and Kevin Wilson." Collectively, the Greek community secretly finished their parade float entry for the mourning AGRs.

On one of the days when the entire AGR membership was away at one of the three memorial services, a neighboring fraternity came into the AGR house to clean their entire home. The fraternity house was scrubbed and vacuumed from the kitchen to the dining room, from the living room to every bedroom and bathroom.

As Mom Dot and the men of AGR gradually came back home, their freshly cleaned home welcomed their return. Sapped from emotional indigestion, hundreds of miles of windshield time, and cursing the loss of life, there was an unburdening sense that others were also grieving.

Approximately one month later, the AGRs dedicated a memorial library inside their house to those three fallen brothers.

As Thanksgiving approached their friends and next-door neighbors decided they should reach out again to let the AGRs know of their thankfulness for their long-standing friendship and assure them they were still in their hearts and prayers. A member of the Sigma Nu Fraternity knocked on the AGR front door asking the fraternity members to come to the front porch.

As the members slowly filled the porch and doorway, the Sigma Nus thoughtfully serenaded those gentlemen still shaped by pain. Likely never before had one fraternity so reverently serenaded another. These were men singing to men, exuding a heartfelt compassion neither fraternity ever expected to offer or embrace.

When the serenade ended there was a stunning silence. A Sigma Nu member stepped forward announcing they were donating a Bible, a Bible stand, and a table for the George, Logan, and Wilson Memorial Library. Those items maintain their historic significance to a legion of men who were and now since have become members and alumni of Oklahoma State's AGR chapter.

Nearly 35 years later, Dennis Slagell the young AGR senior who was the fraternity chaplain in 1977, was asked to read some of the scriptures he used inspiring his brothers to lean on their faith during those dark days following their homecoming tragedy. The AGR house was about to be leveled to make room for a new fraternity structure, so the fraternity had gathered the families who lost loved ones that day ensuring them they would never forget them.

One of the scriptures read was:

Trust in the Lord with all your heart
and lean not on your own understanding;
Proverbs 3:5 (NIV)

THE OSU ALUMNI HOMECOMING PARADE
OCTOBER 24, 2015

THE BATES FAMILY

Early Saturday morning it was still dark in Talala, Oklahoma. The Bates' climbed into their four-door pickup truck for the five and a half-mile drive down to the Oologah-Talala High School parking lot.

Wiping the sleep from their eyes, Paul and Sheri had volunteered to be chaperones and were excited to see their talented 16-year-old daughter, Shelbi, march with her fellow band members. They looked forward to helping with what promised to be a fun day for the whole band. Like most parents, they were proud of Shelbi and wanted to support her efforts. Graduating from Owasso High School in 1984, the Bates' have been married since 1989. Paul previously joked telling people they both graduated tenth in their class. He was tenth from the bottom and she was tenth from the top.

For the first-time ever the Oologah-Talala band director, Mr Matthews, himself an Oklahoma State University graduate, scheduled their band to appear in the big time, Oklahoma State University Homecoming Parade in Stillwater. That nationally recognized and awarded homecoming event is always held in the middle of the fall, in the college town of Stillwater situated in north central Oklahoma west of Tulsa, but nearly a two-hour drive from Oologah. Always looking for new opportunities for his students, Mr. Matthews was excited about sharing the unique experience of OSU's homecoming parade with his students.

Their small town west of Oologah Lake, shares the long ago consolidated school district of Oologah-Talala. Arguably Oklahoma's most well-known actor, humorist, political satirist, and philanthropist Will Rogers was born at the Dog Iron Ranch just outside of Oologah, but Rogers always claimed Claremore as his home since most people couldn't appropriately pronounce Oologah (ewe-le-gâw).

Sheri and Shelbi boarded one of the already warm activity buses, as Paul sipped his hot coffee and finished a brief conversation outside. He reflected on how fast their two older boys Tyler and Austin marched through the same Stallion Battalion Marching Band in the preceding years and how it would be over for Shelbi in no time.

Paul glanced across the parking lot observing the combination of exhaust and steam billowing from another bus and a pickup truck idling, already hitched to a large tandem axle trailer. The assistant band director had already connected his personal vehicle to the school's utility trailer loaded down with band instruments and color guard flags. Like most small towns "it takes a village," and Paul was thankful for the teachers and volunteers of his daughter's school and for someone to drive the trailer-towing vehicle, which made the loading and unloading of marching band uniforms, instruments, and other gear more organized than further stuffing the buses already at capacity.

When their buses and the band equipment trailer-towing pick-up truck rolled to a stop at the parade route's start in Stillwater, it was already almost time for the parade to begin. So Mr. Matthews, the students, and their chaperones quickly unloaded the instruments and cases, then the marching band took their places.

"Have fun, Shelbi! We'll see you at the end of the parade. Love you!" Sheri said.

Giving a thumbs-up, Shelbi shouted back, "Love you, too!"

The buses and the trailer towing pickup headed to the appointed parking spot several blocks away near the CVS Pharmacy parking lot at the last corner of the parade route. When they arrived, a few of the parents made a pit stop in the CVS before heading across the street to the northwest corner of the intersection at Hall of Fame and Main Street.

Initially, Paul and Sheri positioned themselves in a slightly elevated position, leaning against the metal fence next to a drainage ditch that ran under Main Street. Sheri thought it was a perfect spot from which to see Shelbi when she marched through the intersection.

Soon the street was closed to vehicular traffic enabling parade goers to file into the street's intersection along the crosswalk to the middle of the south-bound turning lane. An opening on the east side of the intersection permitted large tractor-trailer rigs hauling floats to exit the parade directly north through the intersection, rather than trying to navigate a tight turn.

While they were standing in that position in the street, Paul spotted a familiar face approaching them.

"Hey, I know that guy. Sheri, this is Leo and Sharon Schmitz," Paul said.

"Well hiiii! Didn't expect to see you guys here," Leo said back.

"Yes, our daughter plays clarinet and is marching this morning," Paul said as the first parade entry was already approaching the corner. "You guys are welcome to watch the parade with us here."

It was the perfect spot to watch the parade and scores of people agreed. It is the busiest, most highly occupied corner of the one mile parade route.

Paul knew Sharon and Leo from the three of them working together at American Airlines for the last 25 years. Though Sharon recently retired from American, Paul and Leo were still long-dedicated employees at the Maintenance Facility located at the Tulsa International Airport.

"Paul and Sheri, I'd like you to meet our son from Houston, Texas, Mark McNitt and this is his wife, Angela," Leo said. "We've been to the homecoming football game before, but they came up to bring us to our first OSU Homecoming Parade."

Shaking hands Paul and Mark, Sheri and Angela warmly greeted each other.

"Well, nice to meet you too, glad you were able to make it up. Hey Leo, you brought that 80 over here didn't you?" Paul continued. He was referencing the MD-80 aircraft American Airlines donated to the Aviation Education program for training at Oklahoma State University, now permanently parked near the taxiway at Stillwater Regional Airport.

"Sure did, that's a great bird for students to learn on over here. Those avionics are the best," Leo said.

Sharon Schmitz and Sheri Bates continued conversations about the parade entries, bands, and some miniature horses that were in the parade. The Schmitz' raise miniature horses on their acreage near Skiatook, Oklahoma, and Sharon was quick to point out their cute, but spunky personalities.

Paul stood next to Leo and Sharon's son, Mark, as together they watched the parade crawl through the intersection directly in front of them for over an hour. More than 130 parade entries make the OSU Alumni Homecoming Sea of Orange Parade one of the largest, not only in the state of Oklahoma, but in the United States. The guys made small talk about the vintage and classic cars, colorful floats, and other impressive entries they found intriguing. Sheri was standing in front of Leo, and Sharon was standing in front of Paul.

The Oologah-Talala Band banner leads the Stallion Battalion Marching Band toward the final blocks of the OSU Homecoming parade route.

Anxious for the parade to start, little 6-year-old Hadley Wyatt was standing with her 8-year-old sister, Mia, and their parents, Sara and Adam Wyatt, of Chattanooga, Oklahoma, as a part of that same cluster in front of the Schmitz' and Bates'. Earlier in the summer the Wyatts had moved back to their family farm in southwest Oklahoma after 15 years of Kansas life. Now, attending OSU events was much easier and would prove helpful in immersing their young daughters in the same Oklahoma State traditions they had enjoyed as OSU students. Their affinity to Oklahoma drew them back to the culture they so deeply treasured growing up.

Earlier seated in her little red wagon, Hadley was now standing with her big sister Mia in the very front of the crowd. They would have a terrific perspective as each homecoming parade float and marching band came toward them. Eventually, it was as though a neighborhood gathering evolved. People nearby made small talk renewing their orange connections and striking up temporary friendships. After all, most everyone there had some association to Oklahoma State University.

At Hall of Fame and Main Street, standing in the crosswalk (L to R, front) are sisters Hadley and Mia Wyatt meeting OSU Spirit Squad Members, Hallie Light and Makynna Edwards, as they finished the parade route approximately one hour before the crash.

Thirty-year experienced Stillwater Police Department Lieutenant John Charles drove the lead patrol vehicle setting the parade pace while Officer Kevin Radley rode his SPD Harley Davidson. Defined by parade protocol, Officer Radley provided additional security presence at the parade's last intersection while Lt. Charles, in his black police department Chevy Tahoe, returned to the beginning of the parade route awaiting all entries to complete their parade start process to bring up the rear.

THE HARRISON FAMILY

The parade was beginning as adult siblings, Kimberly and Kelly Harrison were running a bit late. Quietly slipping out of their parents' new Stillwater home, they were intent to not wake them.

Due to Kelly's late arrival from Lawrence, Kansas, they missed Walk Around the night before, but they stayed up late catching up on her PhD progress in Biosciences at the University of Kansas. A former teacher, Kimberly shared news about a recent bank event and their parents enjoyed their daughters' career passions and positive energy.

Unsure they would even make it to the parade, the sisters' timing was impeccable as they arrived at the last corner of the route to catch the first entry. The lead motorcycle cop, Officer Radley, cautiously glided through the intersection, then behind the crowd standing in the intersection. As he hopped off, the Harrison sisters noticed his handsome, long motorcycle boots and his striking grey goatee.

Initially, they stood on the corner of Hall of Fame and Main Street near the drainage ditch fence. Kelly, a little shorter than her older sister, didn't have a clear view over people standing in front of them, so they moved around the large group of spectators already standing in the street. Eventually, they were standing amidst prime parade viewing real estate where the street was blocked.

They enjoyed the long, festive parade boasting clever collegian creativity. Standing in the cold street with limited physical movement for almost one hour, they were frigid as the parade marched past. Eventually, as close sisters would, they huddled with one another, Kimberly's arm around her little sister keeping her warm. Standing next to Sharon and Leo Schmitz, Sheri and Paul Bates, University of Central Oklahoma student Nikita Nakal, and her boyfriend, an OSU student, Bhardwaj Varma, beside the Wyatt family, and several others, they saw the end of the parade approaching the corner as they stood in the barricaded street.

"The Quapaaawwww Marching Band." Kimberly said with an announcer style voice tone.

"Man, they sound really good for a small bunch of youngins'," she continued.

"I'm cold and kinda hungry. Are you about ready for some breakfast?" Kelly said.

"Yes," Kimberly said. "Should we just run up to Panera and beat the crowds?"

Two Stillwater Fire trucks, a Payne County Sheriff Department vehicle, and a Stillwater Police Department SUV were now in view marking the final entries only one block away.

"Nah, we might as well wait another minute or two while these…" Kelly said something else, but Kimberly didn't hear it.

THE LANE FAMILY

Dr. Gary Lane from Beulah, Colorado, walked north on the sidewalk in front of Hastings with Kaitlyn, his youngest daughter a high school student. They were headed toward Old School Bagel Café, situated one half block north of the Hall of Fame and Main intersection to meet up with his wife, Renee, and their middle daughter, Rebecca, a freshman at OSU. Flying low overhead, two impressive U.S. Military, MV-22 Osprey, tilting rotor helicopter-airplanes chopped the air as the final parade entries approached the intersection. The Lanes stopped walking as eyes nearby looked skyward admiring the hybrid aircraft. The sheer power of these machines temporarily commanded everyone's attention.

Jacquelyn, the Lane's oldest daughter, was a member of the OSU Student Alumni board. A junior at OSU, she retreated to her Stout Hall dorm for a power nap before the football game. Tired from a full week of homecoming festivities and a morning of walking the opening homecoming parade banner down the one mile long parade route directly behind the Stillwater Police Department Escort motorcycle and SUV, she was gassed.

OSU Student Alumni Board members, (L to R), Lucy Lehoczky, Addison Murray, Makenna Gowan, and Jacquelyn Lane, walk the opening banner for the 2015 OSU Homecoming Parade on Main Street.

Jacquelyn had to be fresh for her role in the OSU President's football suite at Boone Pickens Stadium as one of the "President's Partners." In only a few hours she would be greeting guests and helping ensure they knew the football game day routine of the suite level experience.

At the rear of the parade, approximately one hour later Lt. Charles with the Stillwater PD positioned his unit behind two Stillwater Fire Department trucks as parade entry #131, in the final parade slot.

Lights flashing, cruising down Main Street slightly above a snail's pace, again waving at the crowds as folks began retreating from the sidewalk recognizing the parade's conclusion, Lt. Charles was approaching his last leg of his duty at the parade. In only a few hours, he, Officer Radley, and many other in law enforcement, would be stationed at the OSU Football game for the remainder of the afternoon and into the evening until the game day traffic had receded.

THE POPE FAMILY

Alpha Gamma Rho fraternity alumnus Steve Pope and his two granddaughters sat in the Stillwater IHOP that fateful homecoming morning. Steve enjoyed years of homecomings at Oklahoma State with his own parents before actually becoming a college student in 1976. Now, he thoroughly enjoyed sharing the rich traditions with his granddaughters. He wanted them to participate in the growing maturity and life-bonding experiences that come with attending college at a big-time university offered in Stillwater.

The girls were giddy about being in Stillwater with their "Pop." Shortly they would attend their first OSU Football game and they were thrilled with everything engaging their senses. Being in the OSU Homecoming Parade lined with thousands of spectators far exceeded their expectations. Their early morning departure from Loyal, Oklahoma, and riding with their Pop on the OSU Dairy Science Department float left them famished, so now they were all three eating.

Sitting inside the IHOP restaurant on Main Street still warming up with his granddaughters while finishing their breakfast, a tan car sped past the restaurant window headed south. Between bites of pancake and relishing his grandkids' company, Steve thought that vehicle was driving a little fast, but within a millisecond he also decided the parade must already be over and the street must have just reopened.

THE TALLEY FAMILY

The early October morning chill continued gradually lifting as the sun crawled higher into the eastern Stillwater sky. Joyful over his child's first time participation in America's Greatest Homecoming parade celebration, one father reconnected with his daughter near Food Pyramid at the appointed meeting place at the conclusion of the homecoming parade.

Denise and Justin Talley's daughter, Synnove (pronounced Sin-â-vē), had just completed her role in the OSU Homecoming parade on the Impact Cheerleading float with several other area children, positioned near the end of the parade. Their daughter was thrilled to be a part of the Sea of Orange Parade and her parents were just as happy for her to participate.

Hand in hand with his 7-year-old daughter and her friend, Justin approached the Main Street intersection blockaded for the parade. Out of habit he looked both ways. About to reconvene with his wife, Denise, and family friends still consuming the excitement of the final parade entries, the three were halfway through the intersection…suddenly and out of place, Justin heard an engine revving somewhere in the distance.

The three of them held hands as they walked west across Main Street behind the smiling and waving crowd of south-facing, parade goers who were watching the closing moments of the parade along Main Street at Hall of Fame Avenue. Admiring and walking past the gleaming, unmanned Stillwater Police motorcycle unit, the sound of an approaching vehicle caught Justin's attention visually.

He looked up to see a tan 2014 Hyundai Elantra driving south on Main Street in the lane next to the curb approaching the traffic signal at the Hall of Fame intersection. The vehicle's speed concerned him given the amount of pedestrian traffic at the parade just ahead on the same barrier blocked street.

As the vehicle passed the IHOP restaurant in front of the Food Pyramid, Justin noticed it didn't turn, and it was now proceeding in a very "deliberate" manner, not decelerating as it approached the intersection blocked by the throngs of parade goers.

THE MURPHY FAMILY

Both of 6-year-old Emerson Murphy's parents are named Kelly. Her mother is Kelly D. Murphy and her father is Kelly R. Murphy. Emerson's parents were keenly aware of an 8-year-old boy tragically killed after falling from the float carrying Tae Kwon Do students during an Independence Day parade in Edmond, Oklahoma, two years earlier on July 4, 2013.

With this painful knowledge of a child dying in what is supposed to be a celebratory family experience of riding in a parade, the two Kellys debated the pros and cons of whether or not to permit Emerson to ride on the Oklahoma State University Child Development Lab (CDL) float. Kelly D. eventually felt she won the debate agreeing that she would walk beside the float handing out candy along the parade route, so their daughter could enjoy riding in her first-ever parade. Mom would only be feet away from her daughter throughout the parade's entire path.

That morning Kelly R. was still uncomfortable with the idea of the parade, so he opted to go to a tailgate with friends and help get things set up for the pregame gathering across the street from Boone Pickens Stadium. Emerson and her mother planned to be picked up by Kelly R. as soon as the parade was over.

As the Child Development Lab float navigated north, their festively decorated truck and trailer straddled the double yellow lines down the middle of Main Street. Multiple times along her extensive parade hike, Kelly D. saw someone she knew, stopping briefly for a hug, saying hello, or secretly scouring the crowd for a child that maybe none of the other candy distributors noticed.

Their entry was only feet from the end of the route making the right turn onto Hall of Fame Avenue, when Kelly handed some candy to a 2-year-old boy sitting on the curb with his mother on the southwest corner of that intersection. Swinging her bucket with only a few pieces of candy in the bottom, she turned to run across the intersection to catch up with her daughter's float. Spontaneously everything shifted into slow motion.

PISTOL PETE

An OSU junior from Celina, Texas, Taylor Collins, was one of two students portraying the 2015-16 mascot Pistol Pete. He had completed the parade early around 9:30 a.m. having ridden aboard the Pistol Pete Alumni float, entry #9, as the Petes routinely do. Meeting up with his older sister, Kelsy Collins, an OSU graduate now living in Seattle, Washington, they had lots of catching up to do.

They headed over to Old School Bagel Café to grab a quick bite, trading sibling storylines over the next hour. Taylor had been Pistol Pete for six months, so Kelsy had lots of questions about his duties and the various events at which he appears. As the two sat in a booth, munching on bagels, her little brother relayed what an unbelievably fulfilling privilege it was to serve as the ultimate ambassador for Oklahoma State University. Kelsy sat beaming with pride over his maturing passion for her alma mater.

"I'll bet it's exciting on the field with 65,000 screaming football fans surrounding you when something great happens," Kelsy said.

"It actually pales in comparison to some of the experiences I've had. When you visit terminally ill children or an elderly person, now that's fulfilling," Taylor said, revealing a respectful gentleman's grin.

Taylor explained how he does an assortment of appearances unrelated to actual OSU events, such as weddings and private business functions. "Sometimes Pistol Pete is quietly invited to a home or a hospital where there is minimal fan attention. Usually a loved one who is a Poke fan or whose spirits for recovery might be lifted just a little by some Pete love," Taylor said smiling.

"You mean fist-bumping and moustache-twisting?" Kelsy asked. Taylor winked, slowly rocking his head back and forth.

"There are times I've had on that forty-five pound head, looking through the little two-inch painted screens made to look like Pete's eyeballs, and I'm shaking hands with someone who is literally on their deathbed," Taylor paused thinking about one particularly moving experience.

"I've had tears streaming down my cheeks, but since mascots don't speak with the head on, people can't see my true emotion," he paused letting Kelsy take in the image.

"I'll mime as though I'm the doctor," Taylor continued "and grab the clipboard or inspect a computer monitor, nodding positively, or I'll act like I'm inserting a bullet from my pistol in their IV line. Anything to garner a patient's smile or perhaps make the family chuckle."

Kelsy could see her younger brother's passion fueled by this service to others. Clearly, he considered it a reward to portray Pete, but his own ultimate gift was what he gave others.

A few minutes of wonderment spent with Pistol Pete would likely be one of, if not the final, highlight for some of those he visited without ever speaking a word. Those moments were tattooed on Taylor's orange heart. For Kelsy, that icon for OSU was her little brother, and she was simply ecstatic for him.

They finished their bagels and jumped back in Taylor's truck preparing to pull onto Main Street. They were about to turn left away from the blocked intersection, when a speeding police car with lights and sirens flew south directly in front of them. Taylor was the student executive in charge of OSU's Homecoming the previous year, and he knew that an officer charging toward the parade like that meant something serious.

The Stillwater Strong story is one of guiding triumph, resilience, and re-investment, which I believe ultimately highlights how the words of the Oklahoma State University alma mater were never more poignant for us, than they are today:

Proud and Immortal, bright shines your name;

Oklahoma State, we herald your fame!

Ever you'll find us Loyal and True;

To our Alma Mater, O-S-U!

Written by Robert McCulloh
OAMC Graduate '49

Hundreds, if not more than a thousand times, over the last 40 years I've heard and sung the lyrics to that sweet nostalgic music. Arm in arm with family and strangers, we've swayed to those lines. Those words connect us, conducting a bone riveting chill practically every single time I hear them. I'm sure many others experience it too, but those verses and that music strike to the core behind and beyond the purpose of this book. Those words are possibly the very reason this story landed in your hands.

DURING

***

Right Place at the Right Time

CHAOS IN MOTION

Audibly, Justin Talley sensed the approaching vehicle's engine creating an elevating whine as he saw it speeding in his direction. Quickly concluding he was near the target, instinctively, Justin moved into action. As it can when life rapidly and negatively spirals in chaos, time slowed to a crawl. Justin directed his daughter and her friend into the grass, gently sitting them down to not create undo worry. He stepped off of the curb and into the outside lane in front of the parked police motorcycle unit and confidently held the palm of his hand out in a universal "stop" gesture.

The vehicle sped closer to his position near the intersection. Because of the low profile of the compact sized car, Justin could not see the face or eyes of its female driver. However, as an eyewitness, he noticed both of the driver's hands on the steering wheel at "10 and 2," later documenting his accounts to the Stillwater Police Department. This meant the driver was not distracted by one hand being on a phone or adjusting the radio dial, nor was the driver leaning over to pick up something dropped on the floor or from the passenger seat of the car. In the police report, Justin described the driver's body language as "white knuckled" tightly gripping the car's steering wheel.

Justin yelled, "STOP!" and then immediately and at the top of his lungs screamed, "WHOA...WATCH IT! WATCH IT..."

Given the noise of an estimated 1,000 people clapping and cheering at that intersection of the parade, few heard Justin's warning call. The next noises shattered the once upbeat atmosphere. Justin Talley jumped out of the street and onto the sidewalk a second or two before impact, approximately three to four feet from the car's crushing collision with the stationary motorcycle.

The vehicle's black box system, which captures the last running minutes of the car's operations, similar to an aircraft's black box, validated to investigators that the car deliberately accelerated to 59 MPH as it was steered into the parked and unmanned Stillwater Police Department motorcycle unit. The impending commotion was described by many as the sound of a gunshot or bomb.

What they all heard was the graphic, smashing noise of the motorcycle ricocheting from the hood and the windshield of the Hyundai exploding with a gaping hole. Like bowling pins at the end of a bowling alley lane, bodies were lifted off the ground, scattered in all directions.

From somewhere behind him, Paul Bates heard someone yell, "WATCH IT! WATCH IT..."

Paul spun to his left, looking over his shoulder hearing an accelerating engine being fueled to what sounded like maximum RPM's. That noise was someone mashing the gas pedal of the tan Hyundai, then he heard the sound of an unforgettable smashing thud, followed by the ensuing earsplitting chaos.

Now distracted, Kimberly Harrison heard the same noises that seemed out of place. A man's loud voice yelling something almost dueling for decibels over a car's revving engine. She looked over her shoulder behind the crowd.

A speeding car was coming toward them. Kimberly thought it should be turning since it was traveling at such a high rate of speed and the street was barricaded. The car did not turn. Confused by the approaching reality, she concluded the vehicle might unbelievably impact their general area of parade goers.

With no time to explain what was evolving in only a few short seconds, Kimberly began leaning away from the crowd desperately pulling her sister, Kelly, with her. Kimberly yelled, "Oh ssshhh...!"

Everything went black.

THE BATES FAMILY

Unexpectedly hearing someone yell, "Watch it, watch it..." Paul Bates involuntarily turned to his left to see what was happening. Paul turned just in time to see a small car crashing into the parked police motorcycle. Debris scattered as the motorcycle built to "protect and serve" the people of Stillwater was now a deadly projectile being propelled into the mostly unaware crowd of spectators. Responding as if someone had purposely thrown a very large object toward him, Paul automatically turned back to the right, ducked his head down, covering it with both arms.

Every split second seemed like an eternity as Paul's body felt fragments of flying fiberglass, plastic, metal, glass, and other debris pelting him like hail stones. Now peeking between his arms, he caught sight of the car careening inches from him barreling through the intersection. Instantly, the devastation was evident and the shock beyond belief. He thought to himself, "Did I just see what I think I saw?"

Whirling back, he looked where Leo and Sheri had been standing. They were just there and now they were gone. Where were they? The immediate group of people that had been standing and sitting around and in front of them had suddenly disappeared. He seemed to be the only one left standing. His immediate concern was what had happened to his wife, Sheri. Where was she?

Laying approximately ten feet away from where she was previously standing, Paul found Sheri lying motionless and unconscious.

THE WYATT FAMILY

Suddenly, the deafening thud and ruthless smashing sound pierced the air. People standing or walking nearby reactively squinted and involuntarily ducked. The Quapaw Marching Band already beginning their turn east at the Hall of Fame intersection behind the Child Development Lab float ceased their drumming, horn blowing, and marching, and darted out of harm's way.

"Oh my gosh…Hadley!? Hadley…? Mia, where's Hadley?" Adam Wyatt yelled, looking back and forth at Mia, her mother Sara, and the street. Their eyes frantically searching the crowd and even scanning bodies lying scattered throughout the intersection. Frantic, Adam and Sara hoped she had run from the commotion slipping away into the shocked and unharmed crowd.

They found her, however, many feet away lying in the street unconscious with a serious contusion on her forehead and cheek, they knew she had been launched like a rag doll in the midst of this disturbing madness. In that shattered moment, they had no idea what ominous force shot her through the intersection.

Standing directly behind Hadley were both Leo Schmitz and Sheri Bates. The moment the speeding car smashed into the police motorcycle unit, the first people hit were Leo and Sheri. Eyewitness and video accounts verify Leo's body absorbed the initial force of the motorcycle's blunt, disintegrating impact. Instinctively Leo collected Hadley into his arms as they were both lifted off of the ground, catapulting across the intersection.

All three laid seriously injured near one another on the chilly street.

Debris and bodies raining down, Leo, Sheri, and Hadley were just a trio of those critically injured in this mass casualty incident. Nearly 50 victims now lay strewn, checkered across a bed of asphalt, concrete, and even in the grass ditch. Victims and loved ones were screaming, moaning, and crying throughout the corner, but amazingly first responders were only feet away as the parade's last entries.

No one knew it yet, but Leo played a vital role as the wind beneath the Wyatts daughter's wings.

THE MURPHY FAMILY

Turning to catch-up with her daughter's float now exiting the intersection, Kelly D. Murphy felt something take her feet out from under her as they cartwheeled above her head. People were under her and almost reactively they were all collapsing together in the same direction. She didn't know why. She sensed the group of people all landing in a clump, but she landed head-first, slamming into the pavement. These seconds were the fastest and simultaneously, the slowest moments of her life.

Ironically, before a siren was heard, Kelly R. Murphy was calling his wife. He was en route to pick up her and Emerson following the parade at the appointed parent/child meeting location at the Food Pyramid. After having an uneasy feeling about the parade all morning, he thought the parade should have ended by now, and Kelly D. wasn't answering her phone.

Except for those hit or almost hit, for maybe two seconds most of the crowd stood still, frozen by the moment and uncertainty of what had just occurred. Then simultaneously they began scrambling in different directions. The vehicle, which stopped after hitting the curb on the southwest corner of the intersection, was being lifted by several bystanders off of retired OSU professor, Dr. Marvin Stone, who was killed instantly. Sadly, Marvin's wife, Bonnie, also died in the intersection from this same repulsive act. Married nearly 45 years, they were both 65-years-old.

The third victim, a visitor to town that day, also killed instantly now lay deceased in the intersection. Nikita Nakal from India, was a 23-year-old student from the University of Central Oklahoma standing with her boyfriend, Bhardwaj Varma. Nikita, a bright student working on her Masters of Science in Finance, looked forward to experiencing the OSU Homecoming parade. Uneasy with her choice to leave India, her parents still trusted she'd be safe while furthering her education in the United States.

One man was catapulted over the speeding vehicle's sloped hood, summersaulted several feet off the ground, and landed awkwardly on his back directly next to Justin, Synnove, and her friend, Bella Kate Hughes. Wrapped in a blanket and still seated in the grass near a fence and the sidewalk, Synnove witnessed both people and debris showering the intersection, landing in unnatural order. Justin heard the sickening, earthly impact, of the man hitting the ground and saw him crumpled and motionless near his daughter's feet.

Swiftly, the injured man received medical attention by citizen angels nearby who flew into recovery mode. Those people, like many others, happened to be in the right place at the right time and worked to aid the man and countless others. They began speaking to him, asking if he could hear them and doing their best to reassure him that everything would be alright. Though the injured man was flown from the scene, Justin later learned he ultimately survived his serious injuries.

In a panic, Justin scooped up Synnove and Bella Kate, one under each arm, navigating the shocked crowd and unbelievable carnage, trying to shield their eyes from what he knew they didn't need to see. Fueled with adrenaline's strength and emotional weariness, he finally crossed to the Hastings parking lot where he reconnected with his wife and his own parents.

Visibly shaken, Justin reunited with his family still holding one child under each arm. Still wrapped in their blankets, he sat each girl down. "A woman drove her car into the crowd and... she did it on purpose! I tried, but I couldn't stop her," he said.

Aghast at what Justin said, family and friends began assessing the two girls, hugging Justin in relief, wondering why this happened.

Leo Schmitz being assisted by son, Mark McNitt, (left in white hat). Stillwater Emergency Management Agency volunteer Todd Crosby (right kneeling with two bystanders) over Sharon Schmitz lying with her head on a police vest. Seconds earlier Justin Talley asked Synnove and Bella Kate to sit in the grass near the fence in the background as the speeding vehicle approached the crowded intersection.

SIGNAL 82

With no notice, unanticipated and brutal destruction reorganized the parade's last block into an explosion of bewilderment.

Officer Radley had just witnessed his motorcycle hit by a vehicle, launched into the air crashing into pedestrians. Pinching his chest-mounted radio mic button, Officer Radley tilted his head downward. Broadcasting with a blunt candor every officer within earshot of a radio grasped.

"Officer Radley, Signal 82…Hall of Fame and Main Street. We need everything you got!" He said teeth clinched.

The Signal 82 radio call meant a car/pedestrian wreck with injury.

From his parade position, Lt. Charles heard that call on the radio and looked one block ahead toward the crash site. Though he could not see anything resembling a pedestrian / vehicle incident from his position, he flipped on his siren, accelerating past the Stillwater Fire units on the right. He didn't know it yet, but his dash-camera caught the grim evolution of truth and its ensuing pain.

As Lt. Charles approached the intersection in his police cruiser, he witnessed bystanders pointing in the direction of the car and a female lying motionless in the intersection. Coming to a stop, he continued to scan the crowd as the shocking human devastation enveloped the scene. Estimating conservatively, he radioed dispatch requesting everyone available as at least another 30 people were likely injured.

Lt. Charles noted how immediately responsive and unselfish citizens were rendering aid to the victims even before he exited his cruiser. He was struck by the instant and massive volume of people flying into a mode of care.

Two Stillwater Fire trucks (a ladder truck and a tanker truck) were rolling in the parade as entry number #129 and #130. There were four personnel aboard those trucks including a seasoned Stillwater Fire Department medic, Bill Lindsay, riding just ahead of Lt. Charles' police unit. Approaching the intersection, since it erupted right before their eyes, those guys had zero time to prepare for what they were about to see.

It seemed to Lt. Charles as though, in less than two minutes of Officer Radley calling the Signal 82, officials from the Stillwater Fire Department, Payne County Sheriff's Department, Oklahoma Highway Patrol, OSU Police Department, and LifeNet Ambulance services descended to the scene. Promptly congregating with all emergency services personnel, they worked expeditiously as a unified team.

Processing the scene as they had been trained to do, yellow caution tape threaded throughout the intersection restricting access to those who didn't need to be there. That team prepared triage staging to support the removal of victims with life-threatening injuries. Those needing prompt trauma care in that critical window of time known as the golden hour needed to be transported ASAP.

Two Stillwater Fire Trucks parked in the middle of Main Street were homecoming parade entries #129 and #130. Officer Radley's police motorcycle unit lays on its side with multiple law enforcement vehicles in the background. National Guardsmen, Oklahoma Highway Patrol Troopers, Stillwater Police Department personnel, Payne County Sheriff's Department members, LifeNet teams, and others, collaborate throughout the crowded intersection amidst the devastation.

OSU POLICE DEPARTMENT

Lt. Colt Chandler with the OSU Police Department provided parade security, pedaling throughout the north end of the parade route. He was one of three University Police Department personnel on bikes that morning along with four Stillwater PD bicycle officers.

One traffic signal south of Hall of Fame, Miller Street intersects with Main Street. Lt. Chandler watched as parade entry #131 crossed. Post parade protocol directed him to begin heading west towards campus to prepare for the OSU Football game day crowd that had already begun arriving.

A radio transmission popped through his earpiece from dispatch. Lt. Chandler couldn't believe what he was hearing.

"OSU Dispatch, Signal 82 at Hall of Fame and Main Street. Stillwater PD reporting multiple injuries, repeat multiple injuries," the OSU Dispatcher announced.

Immediately responding, Lt. Chandler punched the button on his radio, giving his badge and unit reporting he was turning around.

"Nine OSU, I'm at Miller and Duck. En route to Main and Hall of Fame," Lt. Chandler said.

"Roger, Nine OSU," the dispatcher acknowledged his action.

Lt. Chandler forcefully pumped his pedals back to the intersection he had looped through multiple times over the last hour and a half. He had encouraged people sitting or standing in the street to maintain a safe and comfortable distance from the parade entry traffic. However, it wasn't parade entry traffic that sounded this alarm.

A flurry of other transmissions came across Lt. Chandler's earpiece as he readied himself for what he was about to see at the intersection. No training could have prepared him.

Given the stage of this nearly-ending parade and the multiple first responders placed only feet or blocks from the scene, if this situation had to occur, it could not have occurred at a better time.

Shortly, Lt. Chandler would radio for OSU Transportation to bring one of their shuttle buses to the crash site to help with the mass transport of the walking wounded. That asset provided much needed assistance to the many injured who couldn't walk very far or those needing stitches and x-rays.

Seeing the diverse crowd of people helping one another, Lt. Chandler was profoundly touched. He was looking for those in uniform as he scanned the crowd to see what departments were present. Though there were many, most of those assisting were clearly bystanders who leapt into action.

Inside the caution tape, Stillwater Police Officer, Kevin Radley (left) speaks to an OHP Trooper, while Lt. Colt Chandler (in shorts and bicycle helmet) and a National Guardsmen, give a scene update on their phones, as others work the scene.

Both Officer Radley and Lt. Chandler found the instant outpouring of care from strangers on those corners a testament to the kindness of the City of Stillwater and her citizens. These acts of humanity exceeded ordinary compassion. Life-saving gestures were vital to outcomes that lie ahead, and people were beyond good.

LIFENET

Zach Harris, Senior Operations Manager for LifeNet EMT, served as one of two off-the-truck supervisors that morning. Not in one of LifeNet's four Stillwater stationed ambulances, Zach covered the north end of the parade route. However, at the time of impact he was driving toward a call for a cardiac arrest victim in the parking lot at the BankSNB drive-thru approximately six blocks away.

One ambulance was already on the scene of that situation, but Zach thought he should go since the parade traffic would be proceeding toward campus shortly. He drove one of LifeNet's fast-response units, a four-door Dodge pick-up truck equipped with basic life-saving tools and medical equipment. Without speeding he proceeded south on Husband Street electing not to engage his flashing lights and sirens. Zach was completely unaware of what just happened only a few blocks from his position.

Approaching the intersection of Hall of Fame Avenue, he heard the three "tones drop" on his radio. Fortunately, since Stillwater isn't a major metropolitan city, the occurrence of those three emergency tones being dropped "back-to-back-to-back" calling multiple units is rare, so he knew something awfully big had just happened.

For anyone not involved in emergency services, these tones are the blaring multi-level tones people of a certain age will remember from the hit television show "Emergency!" which aired from 1972-1979. The sound alerts EMS personnel of significant emergencies.

That request came into Stillwater Central dispatch at 10:29:54 a.m., barely one minute after the first call came into dispatch requesting every available ambulance. Zach's unit came to a stop at 10:31:26 a.m., at the intersection perhaps 500 feet west of the crash site.

The dispatcher didn't say what had happened, but as Zach's eyes looked past the intersection in front of Panera Bread and focused on the intersection to the east, he could only see people en masse. He couldn't yet tell what had occurred. As he turned left, he flipped on his flashing lights and siren driving his truck toward the bitter chaos.

Mass confusion, trauma, and people moving in every direction cloaked the scene. It was beyond the scope of anything he had personally experienced. As a trained paramedic and supervisor, he hopped out of the Dodge and grabbed his small bag of life-saving tools. Zach walked through the confusion, assessing needs. Those needs were abundant and immediate.

Like so many, Zach was shocked but pleased to learn Stillwater Police and Fire were there within seconds of the impact. With so many people injured, he had to do a "scene size-up," a relatively quick assessment of what resources are needed in addition to what is present or may be on the way. In that brief 35 second assessment time, given the breadth of what he observed, Zach knew he was in the midst of a Mass Casualty Incident (MCI).

He needed to initiate the "Start Triage Method." This strategic triage process requires spacing four large colored tarps which had been stowed in his truck to help simplify a mass casualty process. These tarps guided injury victims and first responders in that intersection allowing swift and proper medical triage staging.

All emergency personnel are trained on the National Incident Management System (NIMS) standard as to what to do during devastating casualty situations. Created by the U.S. Department of Homeland Security in 2004 in response to what was learned from 9/11, the NIMS provides a systematic, proactive approach to guide departments and agencies at all levels.

The NIMS standard ensures that government, nongovernmental organizations, and the private sector work seamlessly to prevent, protect against, respond to, recover from, and mitigate the effects of incidents. This cooperation is vital regardless of an incident's cause, size, location, or complexity, in order to reduce the loss of life, property, and harm to the environment.

In addition, chain of command refers to the orderly line of authority within the ranks of the incident management organization. Unity of command means that all individuals have a designated supervisor to whom they report at the scene of the incident. On this day, the mutual response and immediate collaboration provided immense stability bearing rapid-fire aid architected within minutes.

Still unsure of what created this situation of mass hysteria, Zach spotted a familiar face in the crowd helping people. Over the screaming and crying voices Zach yelled, "Jason, what happened here?" Former LifeNet EMT, Jason Louthan, now with Oklahoma State University Fire Service Training Center, pointing toward a small sedan with a badly smashed hood and gaping hole in its windshield, "That car ran into a bunch of people," Jason replied. The vehicle rested partially on the curb near the light pole.

The EMTs and fellow first-responders rolled out a green tarp for those injured with only cuts and bruises —— those who could still walk and follow commands. A black tarp is typically used for the deceased, but since this was a crime scene, none of the three deceased victims were moved. A red tarp is used for the critically wounded who need immediate medical attention or they could die, and a yellow tarp is used for other less serious injuries, such as potentially broken bones.

Performing this level of triage onsite saved lives, allowing those with critical wounds to be cared for and transferred from the scene first. Fortunately, Oklahoma Army National Guard Soldiers of the 45th Infantry Brigade Combat Team's 1st Battalion, 179th Infantry Regiment, and 700th Brigade Support Battalion had just finished marching as one of the parade entries. They were vital to assisting in every aspect of life-saving medical triage, care, and crowd control. Whether you possess a deep religious faith or not, no one can deny the providential timing of these vital players in close proximity to this hideous scene.

A bystander directed Zach to assess a critically injured 2-year-old boy, unresponsive, lying in the grass ditch near the Hastings parking lot. Given his larger responsibilities for this Mass Casualty Incident and the severity of the boy's injuries, the EMT knew his scope of need was beyond what Zach could immediately render since he wasn't with sufficient life-saving medical equipment.

Fort Worth, Texas, firefighter Lt. David Tompkins approached Zach explaining he was in town for homecoming and asked how he could help. Zach directed him to the little boy in the ditch. At the same moment, a pediatric nurse approached Zach asking what she could do.

Knowing the severity of the boy in the grass, he directed the nurse to assist the firefighter. That little boy was Nash Lucas, and he would be the first, transported to Stillwater Medical by LifeNet and later airlifted to OU Children's Hospital.

Sadly, after being flown to Oklahoma City and before the day's end, Nash would not survive his massive injuries becoming the fourth fatality of this sad event.

THE LANE FAMILY

Had Dr. Gary Lane and his middle daughter, Kaitlyn, not stopped walking toward the restaurant for that 30 second pause to watch the U.S. Military Osprey, they would have been much closer to impact. The emergency vehicles previously crawling beside them on Main Street as the parade's last entries swiftly approached with lights and sirens shrieking.

Dr. Lane, a board-certified trauma surgeon, has worked in a Level III Trauma Center in Pueblo, Colorado, since 1999. Unexpectedly, he and Kaitlyn were now inside yellow caution tape in a cordoned off accident scene, soon to be turned crime scene.

"Oh my gosh, Dad! That person is bleeding," Kaitlyn said.

Kaitlyn watched a paramedic placing fingers on the victim's neck, then subsequently holding her wrist, but there was no pulse.

"Honey, we can't help her," said Dr. Lane, explaining to his daughter the person was already deceased.

Lane told a police officer he was a trauma surgeon and asked if he could help. Without hesitation, the officer pulled him forward.

A first responder carrying a box of gloves handed Dr. Lane a pair. The doctor scanned the crowd seeking people requiring immediate attention. He shot into action distributing instructions and gauze to loved ones and anyone willing to care for those injured.

As paramedics raced to the scene and then throughout the intersection, Dr. Lane assisted by wrapping scalp lacerations and addressing other extremity injuries to restrict bleeding. He also helped support the already well-organized management team on scene with his triage guidance, confirming which patient he thought needed to be removed from the scene next.

LifeNet EMT, Brandon Quiring, was the assigned treatment officer on the scene. He worked with Bill Lindsay, the Medical Officer with Stillwater Fire. Together they and Dr. Lane assessed critical victims and decided which injuries had the highest priority. Smooth coordination and communication between the various entities on scene was vital.

EMT Supervisor, Zach Harris, assigned Jason Louthan to be transport officer, so Jason and Bill kept track of how many victims were coded as red, yellow and green, deciding, when a helicopter arrived, which patient would be loaded and when.

There were so many moving parts at the scene: assessing the injuries, prioritizing the more seriously injured, and airlifting those most critically injured victims, to receive the highest level of care necessary.

At the scene, practically every piece of medical equipment had been removed from an ambulance nearby. That meant rubber gloves, gauze, bandages, wraps, tape, scissors, crutches, and anything else medically imaginable was being used by emergency personnel, National Guard members, and volunteers caring for and prepping those wounded for transport.

As the visiting doctor rounded with patients in the chilly, devastated intersection checking on 8-10 of the worst injured patients, he was impressed with Stillwater's unselfishness. Though a freak event placed him here to provide care, Dr. Lane felt an overwhelming sense of security for his two daughters, out-of-state students at Oklahoma State. This community-at-large became first responders and virtually everyone was helping one another.

STILLWATER FIRE DEPARTMENT

Stillwater Fire Department Battalion Chief, Greg Connelly a 22 year, experienced Fire Department Captain was the shift commander that day. He was at Station #1 on South Main Street when he heard the same tones from the Signal 82 call Zach had heard.

Climbing into his SUV, Greg began driving from his firehouse toward the incident before the SFD Chief, Tom Bradley knew there was an emergency.

Without the chief asking, he heard central dispatch request truck number three from Station #3. Greg knew the extent of the call must be more significant than a one pedestrian and one vehicle incident.

As he approached the scene, Greg prepared himself for what he might see.

Four Stillwater Fire Stations were still fully staffed as no one was removed from service for the SFD's parade entry. Those two trucks and crews rolling in the parade were only three entries away from the impact which occurred between entry #126 and #127. Had the crash occurred just 5-10 minutes later the intersection would have likely been completely cleared of entries and maybe guests.

Following Greg, Rescue One en route from Station #1 was a fire rescue truck, constructed for rescue outfitted with hydraulic tools and built for this type of emergency support. Approximately twelve personnel were already on the scene from Stillwater Fire.

Since Stillwater Fire Medical Officer, Bill Lindsay hopped off of the fire truck parade entry #130 seconds after impact, he was well into providing triage by the time Greg arrived. Additionally, Colorado surgeon Dr. Gary Lane, Medical Officer Lindsay, and others were determining which victims would be transported next, planning for what is going to happen 15, 30, and 60 minutes ahead as the evacuation progressed.

When Officer Radley saw Bill climb out of his fire truck, he knew they had Stillwater Fire's most experienced medic on the scene. Bill worked the bombing of the Alfred P. Murrah Federal Building in Oklahoma City. Though no comparison of scale, upon arrival Bill also knew this was no routine Signal 82 with a single car and a single pedestrian.

The Incident Command System structure dictates a responder's span of control should not exceed more than seven people and ideally only five people. This unified command means law enforcement, fire, Stillwater Emergency Management Agency, and LifeNet each have their component of responsibility and together they collaborate interagency.

Continual monitoring of each victim's status is key. Since a victim's condition can fluctuate based on internal, head, or other injuries, that ten-minute window of time prior to the touchdown of the next helicopter may change who is next in line. Combined with Dr. Lane's hands-on expertise, Bill's years of experience ensured those most gravely injured were departing the scene in the most logical manner given their minute-to-minute, on-scene triage assessment.

THE BATES FAMILY

The only thing Paul Bates knew at that moment was Sheri was not moving and he couldn't tell if she was breathing.

Drawing a deep breath while kneeling next to Sheri, Paul wasn't prepared for what he found. Her eyes were closed and blood trickled from the canal of her right ear and her nostrils. He tried to focus. He tried to find a pulse. He was trying to see if she was alive, but he found no pulse.

From his training as a Naval Rescue Swimmer thirty years earlier, Paul tried to remember the first thing for which he was supposed to be looking. Speaking calmly and softly to Sheri, she was unresponsive. He knew not to move her neck. Finally, he saw some movement in her chest and could tell she was breathing, but it was shallow. He knew immediately she must have a weak pulse.

Blocking out the growing chaos around him, Paul was wholly focused on his wife. He noticed her head had blood around it, pooling behind her head. Telling her help was on the way, he spoke in a soft, reassuring tone.

"Sheri, babe, can you hear me... I'm right here, you're going to be fine," Paul said.

When she came to after what seemed like an eternity, she groggily began asking, "What happened... What happened?"

Looking into Sheri's heavy, barely opening, and fluttering eyes, with Paul kneeling directly over her, he said, "There's been an accident, you're going to be fine."

"My leg hurts, my leg...it...it hurts," Sheri continued asking over and over, "What happened?"

Two combat boots appeared beside Paul and he heard the male voice said, "Sir, is she alright?"

Not looking away from Sheri's eyes Paul said, "No, she needs an EMT, now." And as quickly as they arrived, the boots were gone seeking help.

Paul said, "We are getting help, babe, just be strong."

A woman with a plaid, purple shirt and purple surgical gloves arrived next kneeling beside Paul. "I've got her head. You can let go now, sir," she said.

Paul slowly and gently pulled his hands away entrusting the woman with gloves to hold his wife's head. It was the first time he realized her blood had not only pooled beneath his hands and across his knuckles, but it covered his palms too and was already on his jeans.

Shortly, a neck collar brace was placed by other medics to ensure Sheri's neck was stable before they placed her on a board to be removed from the scene. Other EMTs and nearby Good Samaritans aiding and assessing so many others, ensured a backboard was brought to Sheri's side. Multiple people worked carefully to strap her to the board in preparation to remove her from the scene.

Once securely strapped to the board, the EMTs gently rolled her over; she was now flat on her back. Screaming out in excruciating pain, Sheri was badly injured. She was taken to the middle of the intersection and placed on a red tarp in the triage area where the most seriously injured were being assessed. Another EMT cut her sweatshirt and placed probes on her upper chest to monitor her vitals. Within fifteen seconds Bill Lindsay said, "she's the next one out."

THE POPE FAMILY

As AGR alumnus Steve Pope and his two granddaughters left the IHOP Restaurant, the curious scream of multiple sirens drew their attention. The sight of numerous emergency vehicles descending upon the nearby intersection several hundred feet to the south of the IHOP ignited Steve's emotions. Every hair on his body instantly froze stiff.

Towering a few feet over his granddaughters, Mia and Saidee, and with one hand on each child's shoulder, Steve's attention remained peripherally on the intersection. He shepherded his granddaughters into his truck trying to distract them with chatter about different words IHOP could spell-out.

"It could stand for, 'I Had Old Potatoes,' or maybe... 'I'm a Happy Orange-hatted Pete...'" Steve said joking. Both girls giggled at their Pop's wit as he continued to try to distract them from the scene beyond the parking lot.

Joking aside, Steve didn't know the seriousness of what occurred across the street. He didn't know if it was terrorism or some other intentional act. He didn't even realize the tan car he saw minutes earlier was involved. He thought maybe a health event caused an accident, but he could tell there were already plenty of first responders at that intersection.

"What's going on over there, Pop?" Mia said.

"I'm not sure punkin, but there's lots of help there. So that's good!" Steve said.

"Oh yes, that is good!" Saidee said.

In fact, at that moment Steve only knew he would attempt to limit their view and knowledge of what had occurred, protecting their innocence. He slowly pulled his truck into the street heading the opposite direction from the scene.

Steve's granddaughters were completely unaware that he had witnessed a tragic scene first-hand at the 1977 OSU Homecoming. Furthermore, they did not know their great-granddad was a college student when President Henry G. Bennett and his wife died in the 1951 airplane crash in Iran. Now the girls would have their own peripheral connection with an OSU tragedy.

Steve would only share the CliffsNotes version with his granddaughters. As facts became clearer, he knew the journey ahead for Stillwater and OSU's recovery would be obstacle filled. A part of Steve's heart and mind flipped back in time. Filled with concern and confusion as to why this happened, Steve knew well the physical and emotional toll this road carried. Recovery consists of potholes and unexpected detours, because that is life. That is what his father and his church family taught him as he digested the ugly reality of his AGR fraternity brother's deaths in 1977 as a 19-year-old college student.

ROB HILL – STILLWATER EMERGENCY MANAGEMENT AGENCY

Director of the Stillwater Emergency Management Agency (SEMA) Rob Hill supervises the massive volunteer effort responsible for barricading intersections and managing traffic flow during the OSU Homecoming parade. Since SEMA gets credit from the National Transportation Safety Board for managing this event as a full-scale exercise, doing their "after action" is an important part of the process. This was the first year the parade staging was moved from 12th and Main, to 9th and Main, so during the debriefing Rob had just told his team how terrific and smooth these changes were thanks to their thorough preparation.

The parade had crawled through the last block of the route when Jim Scott, City of Stillwater Events and Recreation Manager overheard radio traffic of the incident.

"Rob...oh my God. You need to get on the radio and find out what just happened," he said.

The initial report Rob heard from two-way radio traffic was that the motorcycle police officer, Kevin Radley, was hit by a car at the end of the parade. A Signal 82 at Hall of Fame and Main was all Rob knew. Officer Radley's motorcycle, torpedoed by the car's bumper, became a deadly projectile into the crowd. Radley was actually 30 feet away from the point of impact.

For decades Rob's well-trained SEMA volunteer team has provided homecoming route management including intersection closures. Rather than picking up the radio and having something broadcast to radios held by every volunteer, Rob dialed the dispatcher's number, and upon seeing Rob's number on caller ID, the voice on the other end frankly said, "Get to Hall of Fame and Main immediately!"

In a mad hurry to get to the scene one mile away, Rob noticed no one was talking on their radios. He thought that odd until he arrived on scene and the yellow caution tape was raised for his vehicle to drive under. His volunteers weren't talking because they were all engaged in assisting victims and other responders in the massive effort already underway.

Eight SEMA volunteers had been at that intersection helping disperse parade entries through the final intersection of the parade route. Seconds later they bolted into recovery mode. The Stillwater Emergency Management Agency staff, wearing bright green vests, were easy to identify in the various clumps of people kneeling to administer CPR and other life-saving actions.

Rob's team was already engaged in care for what appeared to be fifty victims. To determine the seriousness of injuries, those laying injured throughout the intersection were being asked questions.

As Rob approached he saw every imaginable wound and injury. Witnessing what transpired the SEMA volunteers knew there were also likely internal and head injuries.

"Can you hear me, hon? If you can, blink your eyes. How about squeezing my hand, can you do that too? Good!"

"Now, can you move your arms? How about wiggling all your fingers? Excellent, you're doing just great."

"What about your legs, can you move them for me too? Does that hurt?"

"Okay, now look at my index finger. Follow it…follow it all of the way. Now back…watch it all of the way. Well done!"

If they could follow the battery of tests and other commands, they were graded on their function and responsiveness. A tag identified the severity of each victim's wounds defining areas of complaint for the next level of triage. This action helped in prioritizing the most seriously injured. Applying pressure to bleeding wounds and encouraging those seriously injured to not move until other paramedics arrived to further assess, Rob's guys were amazing under pressure. They shared the voice of calm in the chaotic moments of aftershock.

Called into action by the catastrophic circumstances, those members of the Oklahoma Army National Guard, decked out in their government issued camouflage, had also promptly reconvened in the intersection adding their skilled assistance. Already offering compassionate gestures of kindness, Rob noticed these men and women were in the right place at the right time. These service members train for situations such as this, preparing to be vaulted into selfless acts of kind service at a moment's notice even when chaos and death comes to their front yard. They are however, rarely just feet away when an unexpected Mass Casualty Incident unfolds. Today, they were.

After Rob was briefed on the situation, he gave instructions to his SEMA volunteer team and commanded control of the now cordoned-off quarter mile landing zone next to the intersection. Seeing Zach and the four multi-colored "Start Triage" tarps, he knew the call had already been made to get every available LifeNet ambulance to this intersection. Ambulances from the surrounding communities of Perry, Pawnee, and Guthrie were also requested since they are mutual aid partners.

Rob knew he had a difficult task ahead, but the next one was professionally challenging for him. As he stood in the intersection looking west, he again took his cell phone out and drew a deep breath surveying the panorama of commotion.

Rob thought, "How do I tell my boss that someone breached a barricade at the parade and describe our efforts that quickly accelerated from protecting lives at a fun annual event to desperately trying to save lives without him thinking I've failed?"

He placed that call to the Director of Public Safety, Norman McNickle. Norm was the same patrolman first on the scene at the Alpha Gamma Rho Fraternity tragedy nearly 40 years earlier. At that moment Rob didn't think of Norm as the seasoned Stillwater Police officer from October of 1977. Rob's mind focused on clearly explaining what he knew about this situation.

"Mac, I need you to focus on the words I'm fixin' to say," Rob said.

"Okay," Norm said.

"We are at the homecoming parade. A car drove through the barricades, struck Officer Radley's motorcycle unit. It went into the crowd, and then the car drove through the crowd. I have three to five people that are dead on the scene and dozens that are injured," Rob said.

Norm's words back, echoed the similar shock reverberating throughout Stillwater. "You've got to be kidding me?" Norm knew Rob. His highly-trained emergency management leader was not kidding. Those words just filled empty space. Norm knew no words could adequately provide comfort in a moment of such raw devastation.

"I've got to direct work assignments. Call someone that is not on assignment and get them down here to be your eyes and ears until you get to town," Rob said.

His next calls were to the Stillwater Fire Chief, Tom Bradley, and then the Stillwater Police Chief, Ryan McCaghren. However, with Stillwater Police and Stillwater Fire leadership only feet away, their teams were already on scene.

Rob thought he planned for every contingency of this massive public event. Though he could have done little more to prevent such an event from occurring through the planning, rehearsing, and preparation, at that moment he felt the magnitude and weight of his involvement squarely on his shoulders.

Rob was fresh off a City of Stillwater leadership training and had just finished Tactical Mental Preparedness. In that class, he was instructed how to handle volunteers who have witnessed a traumatic event or scene. Rob's training led him to take a firm approach when watching some of his well-trained volunteers with their heads down.

"Guys, I need you to focus on what you are doing at this moment. This is exactly why our SEMA team meets twenty-four times per year. This is why we drill repeatedly," Rob said. "SEMA exists to serve when the community of Stillwater needs us most. We are needed."

Since the weather was picture-perfect, with light winds, the benefit of having air ambulances involved is they complement the local EMT personnel and resources. Additionally, they provide more manpower and immediate transport to the correct facility.

Rob gathered eight of his SEMA trained men to manage the perimeter of the Landing Zone (LZ). They were to ensure no one crossed through the LZ, the caution tape didn't get caught in the air ambulance rotors, and the choppers steered clear of overhead power lines as they landed.

Original emergency evacuation plans called for victims to be airlifted from the old Cowboy Football practice field east of the OSU Athletic Center. However, the distance of three city blocks to transport the number of seriously injured victims was simply illogical. Looking east on Hall of Fame between Red Lobster and the CVS Pharmacy was where the air ambulances landed to rescue the seriously injured.

After the first helicopter landed and the air ambulance team grabbed their gear and exited the chopper, they began working on the first patient. It became evident rather quickly they needed to get in the air again promptly.

Given the severity of trauma with nearly twenty other victims needing ambulance or air transport, the unified team on the ground concluded they should cease working on the patients in the intersection, load them into the air ambulance, and lift off so other air evacuation units could land and efficiently do the same.

At one time Rob managed four helicopters on the ground loading patients, while two more hovered in the air in a holding pattern. The goal was to keep them as close to the intersection and the victims as possible. The longest period a helicopter was on the ground was nineteen minutes, and this was because a patient crashed as they were loading her and they had to get her stable before lifting off. The shortest amount of time a helicopter was on the ground was just four minutes.

The crushed police motorcycle unit in the foreground, Mark McNitt and Sharon Schmitz sit among other injured parties that could move themselves to the green tarp. Two air ambulances lining Hall of Fame Avenue are readied for take-off in the back of the photo.

The site was efficiently managed as helicopters arrived and gracefully departed like skilled hummingbirds precisely navigating familiar territory. Ultimately, eight air ambulances arrived and departed, delicately landing between power lines and restaurants lining Hall of Fame. Every life evacuated that day was saved but one...the little 2-year-old boy named Nash Lucas.

STILLWATER EMERGENCY MANAGEMENT AGENCY

Deputy Director of the Stillwater Emergency Management Agency, David Casey, worked closely with Rob Hill on homecoming staging. Stationed annually at the Main and Hall of Fame intersection for 15 years, David was comfortable with the strategic direction of the various homecoming floats as they exited the parade. Tractor-trailers requiring wide turns go straight north on Main, children's floats requiring parent pick-up turn east on Hall of Fame continuing behind the Food Pyramid grocery store to meet parents. University-related floats and personnel heading to campus turn left on Hall of Fame feeding them directly toward Boone Pickens Stadium.

SEMA Volunteer Todd Crosby stands in the intersection of Hall of Fame and Main Street shortly before impact.

On this day, David trained his replacement Todd Crosby, a Stillwater resident and a highly-trained war veteran. Standing in the intersection and helping direct traffic through the exit of the parade, Todd's right arm was clipped by the speeding vehicle's mirror as it passed through the intersection. Having personally been involved in service overseas and anti-terrorism exercises, Todd immediately thought the act was just that.

Once the vehicle stopped, his military instincts expected the car to have a bomb, and he anticipated it would detonate shortly, exploding even more debris into the already shocked and horrified crowd of innocent spectators. Thankfully this was not a terroristic act and the car did not explode. That is, however, where Todd's combat-readied mind concluded a potential complication others may not have contemplated.

Crash debris like broken lawn chairs, handbags, shoes, blankets, cell phones, and even a little red wagon littered the intersection and people were sprinting in every direction. Some to help, some to find safety, and like Justin, some to assure innocent eyes didn't absorb the aftermath of what so many had unintentionally just witnessed. The Stillwater intersection appeared as though a bomb had gone off, yet only the individuals standing at the scene knew there was no bomb. In the hours, days, and weeks that followed, no words could adequately explain why this had happened.

Near ground-zero from the multiple points of impact, several people described the sensation with a whoosh of wind and then saw siblings, spouses, and friends literally hurled from their standing or sitting perspective watching the parade. Fortunately, some standing feet away have recounted they never saw the impact, but suddenly their loved one or friend was just gone and no longer right next to them.

Perhaps the absolute shock of the scene that followed erased those images for some, but now what looked like a war zone in downtown Stillwater burned into the memory for others. A reprehensible act so gripping, exposure to Post-Traumatic Stress Disorder (PTSD) leaves not just the injured with wounds.

Courtesy of Stillwater NewsPress

The practically unrecognizable wrecked car intentionally driven into the OSU Homecoming Parade crowd rests on the southwest corner curb of Main Street and Hall of Fame Avenue where it stopped.

ORANGE CONNECTIONS

The last parade entries had passed the parade judges' position so the judges and other officials boarded one of two OSU shuttle buses to return to the OSU Alumni Center. OSU Alumni Association (OSUAA) President and CEO, Chris Batchelder, affectionately known as Batch, had just arrived in a separate vehicle at the ConocoPhillips OSU Alumni Center with OSU Alumni Board Chairman, Phil Kennedy.

The OSUAA Homecoming Supervisor, Melisa Parkerson and the student Executive Director of Homecoming, Hammons Hepner from Freedom, Oklahoma, rode on one of the buses along with dignitaries from the class of 1965 celebrating their 50th class reunion. When the buses pulled into the parking lot Melisa headed in Batch's direction. She had just finished a two-way radio communication with Rob Hill, Director of Stillwater Emergency Management.

Rob, managing all emergency response volunteers, met with all homecoming parade entry personnel two weeks prior to the parade, reviewing the rules and regulations with the responsible parties of every parade entry. His goal is to ensure each participant of the Sea of Orange Parade has a safe and positive experience.

Rob also supervises the planning and security for every intersection of the parade route.

Batch, a long-time friend and Delta Tau Delta fraternity brother of mine, met Melisa Parkerson holding her two-way radio in the south drive of the ConocoPhillips OSU Alumni Center. "I just got off the radio with Rob, and a vehicle breached a barricade at the intersection of Hall of Fame and Main Street. There might be several people hurt," she said. Their eyes were locked.

"What do you mean breached a barricade?" Batch anxiously shot back. Those who know him understand he's just not a quiet or shy guy. Batch stands about 6'3" tall and is a gregarious, teddy bear sort of a fellow who shares an infectious enthusiasm for all things Oklahoma State.

"Someone drove their car through the intersection where people were standing. They don't know if it was a drunk driver or what. We are trying to get more information," Melisa said.

At that moment, another transmission from Rob crackled across the two-way radio. "There are multiple injured, and we do have fatalities. It's like a war zone down here. We are bringing in helicopters."

Immediately, Batch and the official homecoming party heard a distant helicopter, while three OSU Police cars traveling at a high rate of speed blew past the Alumni Center, heading east on University Avenue.

Understandably, Batch thought this wasn't real. He thought to himself, "How in the world could this have happened?" Only minutes earlier he left the stands located in front of the Stillwater Public Schools administration building located at Third Avenue and Main Street.

The OSUAA Chairman Phil Kennedy said, "I can't think of a better time to circle up and say a prayer for those injured and the families of those killed who are going to need it, including us."

Trying to grasp the staggering pain just inflicted, Phil prayed aloud asking God for strength, courage and wisdom as our alumni association would need to take some immediate action. He prayed for the first responders and those providing recovery efforts. He prayed for the healing of those injured and for those who had lost loved ones.

Batch quickly began making assignments so that the OSU Alumni Association staff could be in lock-step with the City and University leadership. Understanding what needed to be accomplished in the near term would be important.

"Melisa, I need your help to calm the student homecoming leadership team. They are just 19 and 20-year-old students, this is a shock to all of us. But they're still kids," said Batch. "Help them get facts to understand where they'll be needed and what they should be doing with this information. I'll get in contact with the city to manage whatever directives and resources they feel they need from us, but first I'm calling President Hargis and Mike Holder. Dear God, please help us all."

Batch's own family flashed through his mind as the enormity of it all sank in. Once he learned they were okay, he had immediate responsibilities to consider and act in an official capacity. Batch began making a series of difficult phone calls, as he reached out to other leaders including OSU President Burns Hargis.

President Hargis answered his cell phone unaware of the chaotic scene which had erupted. Just a little over an hour earlier, as they have for the last eight years, President and Mrs. Hargis had traveled at the front of the parade waving at the same people who now laid injured, stood in shock, or rendered aid to those in need on the four corners of that intersection.

With the few details he had, Batch explained what had happened. President Hargis knew a cascade of other decisions would need to be made soon, so he asked if he had spoken to OSU Director of Athletics, Mike Holder. That was the next call Batch placed.

Speaking with Coach Holder, the long-time Cowboy Golf coach turned Athletic Director, Batch suggested he connect with the University of Kansas athletic officials, the Big XII Conference and FOX Broadcasting officials, because there may be reason to delay the start of, or perhaps cancel, the homecoming football game.

The question on everyone's mind was if this was terrorism, would there be other acts?

Batch then connected with the recently announced, Interim City Manager, Norman McNickle. For many years Norm served as the Stillwater Chief of Police, later promoted to the Director of Public Safety for the City of Stillwater.

Norm was out of state on vacation. By the time Batch reached him, he already knew of the unfolding disaster and was en route back to Oklahoma. Norm confirmed there were fatalities, and the scene had been described to him as looking like a war zone.

"I'm on the other phone, and they just sent out the all call. It's bad," Norm said.

Batch wondered aloud if he should personally go to the scene to console and assist victims, but Melisa reminded him that the Stillwater Emergency Management Agency Director, Rob Hill, explicitly asked that people stay away from that intersection. In addition, with each informational call from Rob, the news just kept getting worse.

Hammons Hepner, the student Executive Director, told Melisa and his student colleagues that his parents had been on the corner of Main and Hall of Fame. He remembered as he and the other student executives passed through that last intersection near the front of the parade, his mom had yelled, "You hoo, HEY HAM!" Ham was an affectionate nickname only his family and high school friends had called him.

Embarrassed by her yelling his nickname, Hammons smiled and waved back at his mom. She had a camera in one hand, waving with the other as his dad beamed with pride. Hammons figured his photography-passionate mother would be there taking photos for the rest of the parade, documenting her son's leadership role in this significant university event.

Now his parents, Monte and Lisa Hepner, weren't answering their phones or replying to text messages and that was not like them. Losing his composure and wanting to be alone, he slipped into a private office in the back of the Alumni Center.

Hammons' inability to connect with his family was deeply troubling and now his peer leadership team felt his anxiety. Excessive cell phone traffic forced calls off the grid meaning some calls weren't being connected. When Hammons finally got the phone to ring and they didn't answer, Hammons was left with questions, concerns and deepening fears.

Hammons' dad, Monte, was a freshman at Oklahoma State University and in the Alpha Gamma Rho Fraternity in 1977, when three students were killed in the last homecoming tragedy.

Not only was Hammons a member of the same AGR chapter as his father, but over the years his father reluctantly shared few details of the painful loss of his brothers in the 1977 incident. Surely his parents weren't in another homecoming tragedy years later.

Twenty minutes of not knowing seemed like an eternity. The phone finally rang. "Dad?" Hammons said.

"Hey! What's up buddy?" his dad Monte said in a chipper tone.

"Are you guys okay, why didn't you answer your phones? What's going on?" Hammons said feeling like the parent.

"We're fine. We left the parade early, just finished a run around Boomer Lake, and left our phones here. We just got back to the hotel. Why?" Monte said.

Hammons, shaken to the core, cleared his throat to regain composure. "Dad, there's been a bad crash involving the parade at the corner of Hall of Fame where you guys were standing. Some people have died, and many were injured. I was so afraid something had happened to you and Mom."

"Oh my gosh, that's horrible," his dad paused. "Well, we're fine."

Worst case scenarios faded away, and Hammons settled down. "Thank goodness, Dad! I'm so glad."

Now understanding the enormity of the situation and its impact on Hammons, Monte gave his son something else to think about. "Are we still set to meet you at Hideaway after the game?" his dad said.

"Yes, that's still the plan," Hammons said.

"Please try to enjoy the game," his dad said.

Still unsure if the game would be played, Hammons and his dad wrapped up their conversation with their usual sign offs. Relieved beyond words, Hammons rejoined his executive committee peers, and they continued to prepare for the awards presentation and other responsibilities, gathering and guiding distinguished guests for their halftime recognition on the football field.

Monte was proud of his son's role in homecoming, and he knew he was looking forward to being in Boone Pickens' personal stadium suite for the game. He felt guilty that Hammons had been so worried, but Monte also knew this homecoming experience would somehow shape his son's maturity even more.

Hammons mind had been there for the last 20 minutes ricocheting through bad scenarios, so he imagined his dad's mind also shot back to 1977, to the same sad memory from years earlier. It was an emotional memory for Hammons having now lived around the same history and their extended fraternity families. The respect those men have for their fraternity's past looms giant. Now Homecoming 2015 had another tragic legacy from which to recover.

Hammons knew other phone calls wouldn't end so positively on this day for others. This was just the beginning of a horrible situation and their executive committee would need to work through some difficult dynamics in the days, weeks, and even months to come.

THE BATES FAMILY

With multiple helping hands, Sheri Bates stretcher rolled into position for placement into the second helicopter preparing to lift-off. As Paul helped guide her strapped to the backboard into the designated space on the air ambulance with two pilots and nurse aboard, Paul heard the radio squawk, the beeping noise of the pilot's gauges and its control panel was being activated. The revolutions of the already spinning rotors were increasing, as a man with a clipboard approached Paul and said, "Sir, how do you spell her name?

"Sheri Bates, S-H-E-R-I B-A-T-E-S," Paul Said.

"And what is your phone number?" the man said.

Paul continued telling the man with the clipboard his number and as quickly as he appeared he was gone, racing toward the next helicopter being loaded. Flooded by emotions with his wife's helicopter now airborne, Paul realized he had no idea where it was going. He ran to a nearby Oklahoma Highway Patrol Trooper. Pointing to his wife's slowly elevating chopper he said, "My wife is on that bird right there, where are they goin'?"

An air ambulance lifts-off of Hall of Fame Avenue while an OSU Police Officer unrolls caution tape, setting up a secondary perimeter near the intersection of Hoke Street and Hall of Fame.

The trooper said, "I'm not really sure, this isn't my normal patrol. The guy on the corner knows the area better than me, check with him."

Paul began sprinting down the sidewalk toward the intersection which was littered by unrecognizable debris; parts of a broken stroller, chairs, and motorcycle pieces strewn throughout the street. Attempting to blink those images from his mind, he approached the next OHP Trooper and while pointing to the flying helicopter explaining his wife was aboard Paul asked the same question.

"I think they are going to Oklahoma Medical," the Trooper said.

"How do I get there from here?" Paul said.

As the trooper provided him the directions of how to get to Oklahoma City, the trooper ended the directions with, "Call *55 when you're close and the OHP dispatcher can help you from there."

Trying to make sense of what happened, Paul's next responsibility was to find his daughter. Mr. Matthews had ordered all of his band students to report to the buses immediately after the crash. Now completely breathless and emotionally spent, Paul rounded the corner behind the CVS Pharmacy and spotted the band students near their bus. Mr. Matthews had already performed a count ensuring each student was present and accounted for, but didn't realize Paul and Sheri were not there yet.

Shelbi spotted her Dad whose jeans and tan work shirt were covered with Sheri's blood. His eyes harbored a deep, unquestionable agony. Speechless, Shelbi looked for answers in her Dad's troubled eyes.

"Your mom has been in a bad accident. She's going to be okay, but I've got to get to the hospital as soon as possible. I'll call you when I get there, but I need you to stay with the band," Paul said.

Sensing the urgency of the situation, Mr. Matthews asked, "What do you need?"

"I need Mr. Gregston's truck to get to Oklahoma City," Paul said.

Before he could start toward the truck another parent overhearing him had already begun to connect the dots. Unhitching the band's utility trailer from the receiver hitch was the only logical option to get Paul on his way to Oklahoma City.

Mr. Gregston, the assistant band director, reached into his front pocket for his truck keys. As the key came out of his pocket a band parent whom Paul had never met before that day stepped between them, taking Mr. Gregston's keys and said, "My name's Julie, I'm driving you...get in the truck."

Hazard lights flashing and truck horn blaring, Paul and his band-mom, new friend-driver navigated traffic as though she were a professionally trained NA-SCAR driver. Zipping south down I-35 they wasted no time driving toward OKC, as the northbound lanes were filled with game day traffic headed toward Stillwater.

During the drive, Paul's thoughts wandered. Should he have brought Shelbi to Oklahoma City with him? He might need her as much as she might need him.

Not knowing if Sheri would be alive when he arrived at the hospital, Paul felt the need to process his family's next moves alone. If Sheri didn't survive, he couldn't bear the thought of Shelbi hearing that news from medical personnel. He felt leaving Shelbi with her friends was the best decision.

THE COLLINS FAMILY

Unable to see anything from the Old School Bagel Café parking lot, the student who portrayed OSU mascot Pistol Pete, Taylor Collins and his sister Kelsy pulled onto Main Street turning right. He guided his four-door F-150 behind the police car, which was racing toward the unknown.

Taylor wasn't able to get any closer to Hall of Fame, so he pulled his truck into the Red Lobster parking lot for a closer look. As he parked facing the mayhem, he noticed a tan car oddly positioned, partially on the curb and in the street.

By the looks on the faces of those in the intersection, he could tell something horrible had happened. People were either helping one another or lying on the ground in unnatural angles. Though he had no idea what happened, a force drew him to that corner to assess what he might do to help.

Taylor and Kelsy now saw the flashing lights of a fire truck and other approaching emergency vehicles. Telling Kelsy to stay in his truck, Taylor crossed the intersection and asked a worker wearing a reflective bright green vest if he could help. That man said, "We need to get some of these people to the hospital now."

"I have a truck and can take a couple," Taylor said.

"Pull it up right here," the man told Taylor as he pointed to the north edge of the intersection.

Hopping back into his truck and putting it in gear, he told Kelsy, "They need help taking some people to the hospital. I'm pulling in closer."

"What happened over there?" Kelsy asked her now trembling hand covering her mouth in disbelief.

"I don't know, but lots of people are hurt. It isn't good," Taylor said as he backed up his truck.

Taylor pulled out of the Red Lobster parking lot and backed his truck into the middle turning lane just north of the intersection. A volunteer on the scene flagged Taylor down, "I've got two injured over here; can you fit them in your truck?"

"Absolutely," Taylor responded.

Opening his truck's rear door and reaching into his backseat, Taylor grabbed the awkwardly-shaped large black bag consuming half of his truck's backseat. Sliding it through the door at the perfect angle, he removed it. Spotting a fellow spirit squad member walking towards him, he placed the large Pistol Pete head, shrouded in its protective canvas cover, on the curb.

"Can you watch this?" Taylor asked.

"Yes, I've got it...GO!" His teammate just happened to be standing near the curb with friends at the parade's end when the crash occurred.

Climbing in, a bystander assisted a 6-year-old boy with a broken leg and the boy's father into the backseat of Taylor's truck. Now there were three people in the backseat and Kelsy, still seated in the front passenger seat, made sure they were comfortable.

Taylor went back into the intersection and asked the volunteer who seemed to be coordinating rides if he needed to take a second victim.

A second victim was identified and this one was a 12-year-old boy. The boy and his mother were carefully assisted into the bed of the truck. Both boys were in significant pain with injuries to their lower extremities. Taylor assured them he would take his time and avoid bumps to get them to the hospital safely.

Slowly piloting his pick-up toward the hospital, it would be a brief six-minute drive. Kelsy asked if she could pray for the boy and his family. She asked for comfort and healing as the boy, his dad, and a new friend they had never met sat in Taylor's backseat. They traveled almost two miles, gradually stopping at stoplights and making calculated, cautious turns as Taylor attempted to create a pillow-soft ride to Stillwater Medical.

To everyone's surprise, when they pulled into the emergency department canopy covered entrance, there were already nurses and physicians waiting outside the doors with wheelchairs. Before Taylor even had his truck in park, the back doors were being pulled open. The two badly injured boys were placed into the arms of caring providers and wheeled into the hospital's emergency department.

It appeared they were possibly the first to arrive with patients and sadly they knew many more would follow. Taylor and Kelsy headed back to the crash scene to see if there were others needing transportation to the hospital.

As it turned out, by the time Taylor and his sister made it back to the crash site, several private vehicles and LifeNet ambulances had already come and gone. Seeing multiple helicopters hovering overhead descending to the site, Taylor began realizing the enormity of the event for which they had just assisted.

When they returned to the location they had left minutes earlier, right where Taylor left it, the OSU Spirit Squad member was still standing guard by the bag containing Pete's mascot head. This brand of orange love may seem uncommon to outsiders, but that's the epitome of the meaningful bond re-defined this day, between Oklahoma State students, alumni, visitors, and Stillwater citizens.

THE BATES FAMILY

Paul Bates in the passenger seat, a band parent he had never before seen was driving him to "Oklahoma Medical." Where that was he didn't know. That was just where the highway patrol trooper said the air ambulance likely took his wife. Headed south on I-35, at times the truck hovered around 90 MPH.

Paul called *55 as directed by the trooper to reach the Oklahoma Highway Patrol dispatcher, securing more information about where they were going and how to get there. Maximizing his thumbing dexterity endurance, the OU Medical Center's automated phone prompts tested Paul's patience. When his cell signal abruptly dropped he was forced to start over emptying the remaining ounces of his attention as they arrived in Oklahoma City. Finally, at the hospital, Paul was advised they weren't sure they had his wife, Sheri. She was indeed in surgery, but because she didn't have any identification with her they weren't sure of her name. She was only registered as "trauma patient number six." Once he was able to thoroughly describe his wife and some of her possible injuries, the hospital staff confirmed they did have his wife and she was already in surgery.

THE MURPHY FAMILY

Sensing something was wrong, Kelly R. Murphy hit re-dial to his wife Kelly D. every several seconds, and still she wouldn't answer, which wasn't like her. Heading toward the children pick-up spot where kids were meeting their parents his mind raced and he didn't even know there had been a tragedy.

Kelly R. would routinely shoot a text to check in and say, "Heading your way." Now since Kelly D. wasn't answering, he was confident something was wrong.

Having no idea Kelly D. had been hit by the car, cartwheeling through the air, hitting her head on the pavement, and landing with two badly broken legs, Kelly R. kept calling. Every child on the Child Development Lab (CDL) float had a parent with them, but no one knew where Kelly D. was. They only knew she wasn't at the pick-up area yet.

Their daughter, Emerson, never saw the commotion of what transpired behind the CDL float. Diana Ross, the director of the CDL, only knew there had been an incident and Kelly D. was missing from the pick-up spot, so the other parents and kids from the float took Emerson to Red Lobster to get lemonade. Diana only had Kelly D's phone number, so she hoped Emerson's dad would arrive soon. Kelly R. knew none of this.

Finally, a first responder assisting Kelly D. while she lay in the intersection unconscious with two severely broken legs removed her ringing phone from her jean's back pocket and saw on the screen, "ICE Kelly." When another voice answered, not his wife's voice, Kelly R's heart sank to the pit of his stomach.

"Hello," the voice said.

"This is Kelly, where is my wife?" Kelly R. anxiously shot back to the voice on the other end of Kelly D's cell phone.

"I'm here with a woman that may be your wife. There has been an incident. Get to the intersection of Hall of Fame and Main as soon as you can," said the voice on the other end.

"Where's my daughter?" Kelly R. said, inhaling and holding it.

"I'm sorry sir, there are multiple people injured here, and I don't know anything about your daughter," the voice replied.

Frantic and wrought with anxiousness, Kelly R. arrived on scene. Blown away by the chaos, he went from person to person lying in the street looking for his wife and daughter while surrounded by helpful citizens.

Locating his badly injured wife, he couldn't believe his worst fears, were now a sickening reality. With mounting anxiety, Kelly R. looked across the intersection at the other victims. He didn't spot anyone else he knew from the CDL float, and no one seemed to be looking for either his wife or Emerson.

Given their dialog about the unfortunate Edmond parade fatality involving a child, Kelly R. had already imagined the fear of losing their only child in some freak incident. The possibility of becoming a single parent or losing his wife and daughter was beyond comprehension. He couldn't lose the love of his life and the one they brought into the world.

First responders concluded that given her serious head injury, a compound fracture with one bone peeking out from her ripped jeans, and the other leg also smashed in multiple places, Kelly D. would need to be transported by air ambulance.

Kelly R's parents received the call advising them of Kelly D's involvement in the crash. In town for the game, they rushed to the scene to see how they might assist in finding their granddaughter, Emerson.

Because they were not immediate family, they were not permitted inside the crime scene area. As they stood gawking at the view from behind the yellow caution tape, no one except the CDL float participants knew Emerson was only feet away waiting inside the Red Lobster.

Kelly D. was laying critically wounded with chaos all around her, and the Murphy's daughter had to be found. She needed to be told her mom was seriously injured. It would be hard for Emerson to wrap her young mind around the reality of this, since the parade was supposed to be something fun for every family.

Finally, one of the Murphy's neighbors connected with Diana, the Child Development Lab director. Distracted by the circumstances Diana answered a number she didn't recognize.

"Hello, this is Diana," she said.

"Hi Diana, I'm a neighbor of Kelly Murphy's and I heard you're trying to reach her husband Kelly, would you like his cell phone number?" the voice said.

"Oh yes, thank you so much," Diana said.

Quickly concluding that conversation, Diana connected with Kelly R. telling him that his daughter was fine and with other children from the CDL float. The kids were unaware of the harsh circumstances outside Red Lobster's front door.

They made a plan to meet at the YMCA parking lot several blocks from the crash scene. Kelly R., his parents, and Emerson could be reunited away from the congestion and chaos. When her dad arrived and emerged from his car, already waiting at the YMCA, Emerson sprinted into his open arms.

"Hey Daddy!" Emerson said, as Kelly R. hugged her for several seconds, not wanting to let go and not wanting to explain this cruel reality. He took another deep breath.

"Punkin, I need to tell you something," Kelly R. said as he looked sweetly into his daughter's precious eyes, his own now welling with tears.

"Mommy got hurt at the parade, and she had to go to the hospital," Kelly R. said. Not fully confident of the level of detail he needed to share, he also didn't want her to hear stories later from other children or someone who talked about those who died.

"Can I go see her? I mean she's going to be okay, right?" Emerson asked sheepishly.

"Babe, she and some other people got hit by a car, and she hurt her legs and hit her head. She's going to get the best care possible," Kelly R. stopped talking with a lump in his throat.

Looking into her dad's eyes she sensed his anguish, not expecting his response and the harsh seriousness of it all, Emerson felt a wave of nausea and unexpectedly threw-up. No amount of tenderness softened the sting of his explanation.

Reaching inside his car, Kelly R. grabbed a bottle of water so his daughter could rinse her mouth. The sickness of her Dad's unexpected words began to be diluted as they again embraced, and he told her they could pray for her to get better.

As Kelly D. was airlifted to Tulsa, she drifted in and out of consciousness, remembering only the slightest bits of the actual trip and the kind faces accompanying her while airborne. When the air ambulance originally lifted off it was headed to Oklahoma City, but since other victims with similar injuries were already arriving by helicopter at OU Health Center and Mercy, they didn't travel too far before being diverted to St. John's Hospital in Tulsa.

Once at the Tulsa hospital as she was being prepped for surgery, a nurse asked Kelly D. if she could recall her mother's phone number. Possibly as a tactic for distraction as they cut away her jeans, she verbally recalled the correct phone number, which was music to the nurse's ears.

Over the next few days she had multiple CT scans done on her head and was x-rayed and examined more times than she could count. She remembered very little about the actual impact or the next few days of recovery.

Though Kelly D. would learn much later, the doctors had said no television, no phone, and limited interaction with people outside of immediate family allowing her brain needed rest. A loving family member strictly screened her visitors. Later Kelly D. felt she needed to apologize for the compassionate tactical stonewall, but her friends understood her critical condition.

Her memory was like a bad cell phone connection with periods of indecipherable and lost minutes. Kelly remembers only a handful of sporadic seconds before and after impact. It was days before anyone would actually tell her what had happened.

As it turned out, Kelly D's compassionate heart trying to give away the last few pieces of candy in the bottom of her bucket, placed the final, fully healthy steps of life into the path of a speeding car.

THE HARRISON FAMILY

Now waking up on the pavement, Kimberly Harrison had hit her head hard on the street. At a minimum, she had a bad concussion and a shattered knee cap. As people rushed to her aid, Kimberly tried to sit up and began telling people she was okay.

"Seriously guys I'm fine. I just need to walk this off...I'll be okay, I just need to find my little sister."

"Kelly, where are you?" Kimberly said. "Kelly?"

"You're not fine, you've got a bad leg injury ma'am. Please lay back down," a calming voice said.

"I'm okay, just please let me try to walk this thing off and find my sister," Kimberly said pleading with the growing number of kind-hearted voices offering aid.

Amid the moaning and crying crowd, Kelly lay only a few feet away, overheard the banter evolving between her sister and people trying to help. Kelly gawked at Kimberly's broken leg.

Trying to distract herself from her own mangled mess with two broken legs, Kelly literally chuckled to herself. "Whoa now, Sis, you are not walking that off!"

Kelly knew she, too, was in bad shape. People she had never before seen were holding her hand telling her help was on the way.

"We should have gone to Panera," Kelly thought.

Given the extent of her leg injuries, Kelly was loaded into one of the eight air ambulances coming and going. She was headed for a trauma center, but which one?

Kimberly didn't know where Kelly was going, but as she was loaded into the bed of a pick-up truck she reached for her cell phone. It wasn't in her hoodie pocket.

She needed to call her Mom and Dad. They would be devastated.

As Kimberly arrived at the hospital, her parents received a phone call from her phone. A Guardsman from the Oklahoma Army National Guard found the cell phone in the intersection among the debris and called the number that said, 'ICE Mom.'

Little did Kimberly know when she entered her mom's contact name, that the 'In Case of Emergency' acronym would assist a first responder in an actual emergency.

Seeing Kimberly's number pop up on her caller ID, her Mom answered.

"Hi, Boo, how was the parade?" Suzie Harrison said, cheerfully answering her phone, calling her by her long-used family nickname.

"Ma'am, I'm with the National Guard, and I found your daughter's phone in the street. There's been a pretty bad accident at the parade up here on Main Street. I'm not sure who your daughter is or if she knows she lost her phone," the Guardsman said.

Now panicked from this unexpected call, she knew Kelly was with her. Knowing they would be connected at the hip if something bad happened she just knew they were together.

But why hadn't Kelly called them yet?

"They are flying people from the scene, and they are taking several by ambulance to Stillwater Medical. If you don't hear from her soon you might want to call the hospital. I'm just in town for the parade and am staying at the Wyndham Hotel. I'll leave this phone at the front desk and you can pick it up when convenient," the Guardsman said.

"I'm sorry I don't know anything more. I do hope your daughter's okay."

Suzie and her husband, David, immediately headed to Stillwater Medical Center concerned for what they would find. During the drive, they repeatedly dialed Kelly's cell phone, but each time voicemail intercepted the call.

STILLWATER MEDICAL PHYSICIANS AND TEAM

On this Saturday morning the Medical Director for the Emergency Department (ED) at Stillwater Medical Center, Dr. Charles Olson, and the ER staff had experienced what they would deem a relatively light morning in patient volume. Only three emergency rooms had patients in them, and each were in the process of being moved to other locations of the hospital having been triaged and their care initiated.

Dr. Olson was scheduled that day to be a volunteer physician on the sidelines for the Oklahoma State vs. Kansas football game, which he has regularly done since 2007. His game-time job positions him to help provide medical attention with OSU's Head Team Physician, Dr. Val Gene Iven should anyone involved with the game have an injury or health event. However, as is his routine, Olson stopped by the hospital first to check the "patient tracker."

The patient tracker includes names of patients in the ED, their issues, stability status, and timeline process of admittance or discharge. He checks to ensure adequate resources and then typically departs for the game.

A typical game day includes various falls and health events associated with having an increased visitor population in town. So, at the conclusion of each football game, Dr. Olson normally returns to the ED to check in again.

Dr. Olson has been an emergency department physician at Stillwater Medical since 1999. Before that he was at St. Anthony's Hospital in Oklahoma City and happened to be in their ED on April 19, 1995, the day of the Murrah Building bombing. Dr. Olson's deep faith and seasoned ED team, enabled him to deal with the aftermath of that catastrophic event when victims poured into St. Anthony's emergency rooms. He also teaches urgent and trauma care situations and has been a ten year, Stillwater Police Department - SWAT team physician, and a Disaster Medical Assistance Team physician.

A nurse attending the OSU Homecoming Parade incident called the hospital to prepare them.

"There appear to be at least seven red patients (meaning significant injuries urgently needing care), multiple yellows (meaning broken bones and potentially serious injuries), and multiple greens (meaning soft tissue wounds including lacerations and possible fractures)," she said.

Most likely none of the patients or their families in the hospital knew the vast training and experiences Olson and his ED team possessed, but they truly were in gifted hands thanks to the intense training and preparation of those nurses and physicians surrounding them. In a small city like Stillwater, news travels fast and there were ample assets surrounding the emergency department and multiple others inbound to prepare for the arrivals of the injured.

As the fifteen individual emergency rooms filled up, Olson and the administrator on duty, Denise Webber, directed two more areas adjacent to the ED be opened to care for the less seriously wounded. Those patients with superficial wounds were taken to the Endoscopy and Infusion Suites of the hospital to accommodate the volume of patients, including those without life-threatening injuries.

As patients began arriving, emergency physicians Dr. Eric Williams and Dr. Stuart Shoemake, were deep, in patient care. The first three patients were the youngest, each with serious injuries, so the staff knew they would be transferring them on to OU Childrens' Hospital for a higher level of care.

As other patients began arriving, Dr. Olson said to the staff, "We need to get Dr. Baker here. In fact, we need Dr. Baker and all of his partners right away," referencing the three other general surgeons, and partners in the same practice.

They were all needed to help assess and initiate surgical restoration and could help the victims begin their roads to recovery. Within minutes of learning about the crash, nearly twenty local physicians flocked to the hospital.

THE BUS

OSU Spears School of Business student, 20-year-old Joe Bailey grew up with an appreciation for what it meant to have a Commercial Driver's License. He proudly watched his dad crisscross the country in an 18 wheeler, so he understood the subtleties and responsibility of driving something larger than the average passenger car or truck.

As a Student Supervisor for "The Bus," Joe had driven a shuttle bus for the community of Stillwater and Oklahoma State University for nearly three years. On game days he would typically shuttle many of the same passengers from the OSU Posse Parking Lot at the Stillwater High School Football Stadium to Boone Pickens Stadium. On October 24, he expected heavy traffic since the morning's parade blocked off a one-mile stretch of town.

Joe's OSU Parking and Transit supervisor, Derrick Mooney, placed great faith in his Student Supervisor. As usual, Joe and several of his colleagues arrived to work early at the Compressed Natural Gas Fuel Station, located at the intersection of Lakeview and Western near the south edge of the Stillwater Regional Airport. Joe just finished his "pre-tripping check," a required walk around the 2010 El Dorado – International, Easy Rider 2 when Mooney, as they call him, asked Joe to drive to the corner of Hall of Fame and Main Street.

"There's been an incident near the parade," Mooney said. "I need you to pick up the walking wounded and shuttle them to the hospital."

Joe had never had that kind of a request before. He knew that was a nice pat on the back from his boss, so he jumped in one of the approximately twenty orange, white, and black (CNG) buses known throughout the community as "The Bus."

Joe pointed his 36-passenger bus south to Main Street unsure of how many riders he would have, his total seating and standing capacity was 45-50 people, depending upon the riders' sizes.

As Joe slowed near the intersection, his jaw dropped. He saw a massive scene of people standing and kneeling in the intersection. First responders were pointing, and people were crying. Colored tarps were laid on the ground amid a flurry of activity. As he came to a stop, Joe heard helicopters overhead. It was like a war zone and nothing he had ever seen.

A Stillwater firefighter approached the bus door.

"Let's park this thing next to that fire truck," the firefighter said. "We want to position you to get as close as possible to the victims."

Maintaining his composure and focusing on the firefighter, Joe peeled his eyes away from the trauma. He had a job to do.

As soon as he parked the bus, approximately fifteen people lined up at the doors. Tear streaked and wide-eyed faces held one another ready to load. Joe noticed a few victims with obvious leg injuries.

He exited the bus to lower the secondary door's hydraulic wheelchair ramp. As Joe offered his hand to the riders, he recognized that most were suffering from bruises and broken bones. From what he could tell, none of the passengers were bleeding and none appeared to be in mortal danger.

About thirty people were now seated on the bus approximately half were injured, while the others were family members or friends who had just finished the parade, bounding into action in the right place at the right time. Several Guardsmen helped wherever they were needed assisting people as they got situated. A couple of them stayed on the bus visiting with people while they were waiting to depart the crash scene.

It had only taken about five minutes to load the bus, but it was another anxious 20 minutes to get the all clear from the crash site. Emergency personnel wanted to make sure there were no other walking wounded needing transportation from the scene.

When the all clear was given, Joe carefully put the bus in drive, trying not to jostle his delicate cargo and headed to Stillwater Medical.

In a Mass Casualty Incident, there are certain protocols to be followed to ensure that certain resources aren't taxed. But Joe didn't know that, and no one told him. The directions were supposed to be given to transport these victims to the Perry Memorial Hospital 24 miles west in Perry, Oklahoma, but given the confusion and chaos at the scene, that directive was not given and Joe headed to Stillwater's hospital.

As the bus moved, chatter among the passengers began as they recounted what had just happened, and tried to make sense of the chaos and devastation. Joe was trying desperately to avoid bottlenecked traffic and blocked streets. With many injured passengers aboard, Joe was extra cautious to not brake suddenly or turn abruptly, trying to complete the two-mile trip with as little jarring and jolting as possible.

He headed north to McElroy, then south down Duck Street, arriving at the hospital via an unconventional route. The hospital entrance off of 7th Avenue was closed to traffic, making room for an additional helicopter landing zone in the parking lot at Stillwater Medical. Joe had to drive around the block, entering from 6th Avenue, then finally pulling into the ED's circle drive, he parked the bus.

Joe manned the hydraulic wheel chair ramp and slowly lowered each of those unable to step down stairs. As the hospital doors opened, Joe was overwhelmed by the staff and family members who were there to greet the injured and assist them as they walked in. Several provided wheel chairs for those having difficulty walking.

From the crash site to the hospital, strangers helped strangers and did all they could to alleviate pain and hardship. Joe knew he was experiencing something that would stay with him all the days of his life.

Before pulling away from the hospital he did a walk-thru of his bus to make sure no one was left behind. He checked for medical supplies, bloody gauze, or seats which may have needed cleaning.

Before departing the hospital parking lot, Joe took a deep breath and radioed Mooney.

"Mooney, you got a copy?" Joe said.

"I'm here," Mooney said.

"I've taken the victims to the hospital. Do any others need transport?"

"The site is clear, Joe," Mooney said. "Go ahead and run your regular football game route."

Joe proceeded to the Stillwater High School football stadium parking lot to begin shuttling fans in the Silver Star Posse Parking to Boone Pickens Stadium. He arrived about 45 minutes later than normal and since he had driven that route every game of the season, his regular riders wondered where he had been. Reluctantly, Joe shared an overview of his delay as their pregame excitement turned into dismay.

THE PETTY FAMILY

A friend told me once, "When your mother calls always answer. She won't always be there for you." I certainly know with two college age children, I feel the same way about their phone calls. I won't always be there for them, and they may not always be there for me.

Our daughter, Catherine, was a sophomore at Clemson University and had returned home for a long weekend to see our family, her friends, and enjoy our homecoming parade which she has done for most of her previous 20 years having been born at Stillwater Medical, in October of 1995.

Courtesy of Stillwater Strong

*Born the weekend before the OSU Homecoming in 1995, our daughter Catherine has attended prac-
tically every OSU Homecoming Parade since. In 2001, a then 6-year-old Catherine hugging her
Grandad, David Petty, and me.*

For over 40 years the OSU parade and homecoming celebration has been part
of our Petty family tradition. This year would be no different. We would gather to see former classmates and friends who infrequently make the trip back to
our cool college town. Walking down the street or sidewalk, people frequently
nod politely, say hello, and even fist-bump or hug and say, "Go Pokes."

Approximately forty-five minutes earlier, as I had done each of the last 30
years at homecoming, I waved at alumni and guests on that prominent corner.
I was perched aboard our Pistol Pete Alumni float trailer, carrying the current
day Pistol Pete and alumni who have served as the university's mascot.

I was just one of about twenty guys on that trailer waving at parade-goers.
Eighty-eight students have been the pistol-packin', headgear wearin' icon for
the Cowboys, and as Pete #40, it was an honor to serve as mascot during two
years of my college career.

Courtesy of Leo and Sharon Schmitz

*Alumni Pistol Pete Float photo taken by crash victims Sharon and Leo Schmitz from their position in the
intersection of Hall of Fame Avenue and Main Street at approximately 9:15 a.m. Just 75 minutes before
the crash.*

Our mascot alumni group are always positioned early in the parade sequence with the OSU Spirit Squad, so the current Pistol Pete and the rest of the squad can prepare for their other appearances across campus prior to kickoff of the football game. Some of these participants typically watch the other parade entries as they exit the parade route at that exact same corner at which they conclude the approximately 130 entry parade every year. It would be that corner where lives were forever altered.

As we were shuffling family cars following the homecoming parade, my phone rang. We planned to do the thing we did at the conclusion of every parade, drive a block or two away and drop my parents off at their vehicle before some tailgating with old friends prior to the homecoming football game.

"Hi honey, what's up?" I answered as I saw it was my daughter calling. Having her home from college is always enjoyable for our family and the fact she got to visit with my aging parents and watch the parade with them was a nice bonus.

"Dad, I think something terrible happened. Do you know what's going on?"

I could tell from my daughter's voice she was more upset than she could clearly articulate. Completely unaware of what had occurred I said, "No, where are you, babe? What's happening?"

Catherine had seen terror in the eyes of those moving away from the scene and coming in her direction, those who had previously been sitting and standing near that fateful intersection.

"People are coming toward us sobbing. They have shocked looks on their faces," Catherine said.

Hearing the concern in my daughter's voice put a lump in my throat. What if this call was coming from her while she was at school in Clemson, South Carolina, nearly 1,000 miles away?

My mind erratically checked off audacious scenario boxes. I thought maybe someone had fallen from a float, or perhaps worse someone crossing the street had been hit by a parade vehicle. However, her description and grave concern led me to believe maybe it was even terrorism, or perhaps a shooter. One's mind tends to jump to worst case scenario quickly in a situation like this.

"I think you should go a block or two over to avoid the crowds. I hope it isn't something serious," I said.

Though my fleeting thought of an active shooter seemed doubtful, I never imagined the truth could be equally significant. I didn't want my daughter to see or experience whatever the panicked witnesses saw.

On the way home, I called Shyla Eggers, the Director of Public Relations at Stillwater Medical, the same hospital for which I manage the Stillwater Medical Foundation. "Was there an accident at the parade?"

"Oh Scott, it's bad. At the end of the parade route a barricade was breached. It sounds like there are fatalities and multiple injuries. The 'all call' has been made to get medical personnel to the hospital immediately," Shyla said.

"Oh my gosh. Do you need me to do anything for you?" I said

"We may need help with the media and visitors. Yes, please come if you can," Shyla said.

At that moment, I saw a helicopter zipping overhead as I turned the car into my neighborhood, not an uncommon site on the day of a Cowboy Football game, or OSU's Homecoming when often 70,000 alumni, students, family members, and visitors flood the streets for the festivities. Seeing an Oklahoma City television station chopper in the sky on a day like this was not surprising, or so I thought. However, Shyla's words and the seriousness of her tone suggested otherwise.

As I walked into my house, I told my wife, Gerri, "I guess Catherine's right, there has been a pretty bad incident near the end of the parade route. They want all on-call medical personnel at the hospital. I'm gonna head that way."

Gerri looked puzzled asking, "So, why are you going?"

"Shyla said she may need help with the media, so I'll just see what I can do and help however I can. I'll tell people what I'm told to tell them," I offered with some uncertainty, since I had no earthly idea of the magnitude of the situation. "I'll meet up with you at the game, if I stay at the hospital that long," I said. In my wildest dreams, I couldn't imagine the intense patient barrage SMC actually faced in the minutes ahead.

Though I have no formal medical training, each year as a Stillwater Medical employee I take about twenty-five different short online tests. Passing ensures our employees and management team knows what to look for in the case of emergencies, unique situations, or catastrophic events. It also educates us on how to respond in complex situations and educates on the importance of confidentiality in all health matters. However, nothing could have truly prepared me for what I was about to encounter.

STILLWATER MEDICAL

Orthopedic surgeon Dr. Tom Wuller had already been to the hospital, completed his rounds, and returned home. As the on-call orthopedic doctor, he began receiving text messages and calls from friends about the parade incident. Before he even received an official call from the hospital, Dr. Wuller kissed his wife and headed to Stillwater Medical.

A conscientious, 20 year experienced surgeon, Dr. Wuller and his partners have seen their fair share of broken bones from car wrecks, bad falls, and a variety of other orthopedic related traumas. Except for the fairly infrequent multiple injury automobile accidents, not often are the Stillwater doctors thrust into caring for numerous severe patient injuries in the emergency department.

When Dr. Wuller arrived at Stillwater Medical, he observed Dr. Olson already seeing patients, but there were only a couple of victims that had arrived. The earliest injured patients arrived by private vehicles, but shortly thereafter, multiple ambulances and eventually, "The Bus," loaded with walking wounded arrived, flooding the Stillwater Medical emergency department and waiting room.

Anyone working in healthcare understands what the onslaught of a bus load of injured and other able-bodied passengers being brought to the hospital all at once would mean. The time to register, process, triage, x-ray, and review information could take hours to complete if staffing levels were normal. Thankfully, staffing levels grew exponentially as the patients arrived.

Dr. Wuller, now wholly focused on going from patient to patient, wasn't fully aware of the increasing number of patients arriving. As he glided room to room ordering x-rays and other medical tests and prescribing medication throughout the fifteen exam rooms in the emergency department, the activity and human census ballooned substantially. Now his own patients were evenly spread throughout the ED, which is a horseshoe shaped area approximately 20,000 square feet in size.

X-rays were being digitized on patients as the staff began rolling the mobile x-ray unit to and from all fifteen rooms where needed. Like clock-work the physicians, nurses, and techs transitioned to paper charts rather than using the electronic medical record to expeditiously document, triage, and prepare patient orders for care. Paper charts were simply more efficient given the patient needs and the force of 'all-at-once' care.

Drs. Wuller and Baker both performed surgery on Kimberly Harrison that day. CAT scans showed a fluid build-up around her lungs and abdomen.

Like sweating externally in the heat of a hot summer's day, the body also excretes fluid to protect internal injuries. Externally and internally, Kimberly's body was badly injured by two impacts. One, as she was thrust by the car's contact and two, from her rough landing in the street.

With confidence and concern, Kimberly asked the surgeon about the fluid.

Pointing to her abdomen area she said, "So Doc, give me the best and worst case scenario with this fluid build-up."

"Best case scenario – it is only fluid that rushes to the area to protect it. Worst case scenario – you have bleeding or some other trauma requiring us to remove some of your intestines." Dr. Baker paused to let that news be absorbed.

"So that's it? You just might have to remove some intestines and that's not a very big deal?" Kimberly said.

"There is a possibility you may have to be on a colostomy bag for a few weeks or few months during recovery, depending upon surgical outcomes and healing," he said.

"Okay, I just needed to know where we stand," Kimberly said.

Before rolling into surgery Kimberly barked a final request of pressing importance. "Mom, keep an eye on that OSU game. I want to know how my Pokes are doing!" Kimberly said.

"Oh Kimberly, give me a break. You're going in for emergency surgery," said her Mom, rolling her eyes.

"I'm serious, Mom. I want to keep up with it," Kimberly said again.

"Okay, I will. You just be a good patient," her Mom said, kissing her on the forehead.

Thankfully, the exploratory surgery validated the fluid as indeed only fluid. The knee repair, however, would take time in a wheelchair and months of physical therapy from which to recover.

Dr. Wuller never ventured to the hospital areas covered by other physicians, dealing with mostly soft tissue injuries, which had arrived via private vehicles or The Bus. In the ED, he evaluated numerous fractures, tendon injuries, and muscle tears, mostly in the lower extremities. Ultimately, a patient's positive attitude and will to heal drives the speed with which one physically and emotionally recovers.

Given the demands commanding hospital staff attention, it was late in the morning before Dr. Olson grasped the depth of the situation when he was tapped on the shoulder by Dr. Suzanne Burks, Director of University Counseling Services. Next to her stood Dr. Lee Bird, Vice President of OSU's Student Services. Both women have dealt with and counseled those dealing with tragedy, and the impact to both the University and Stillwater would once again be hefty. In fact, this event was the largest single event in emergent care operations the hospital had ever encountered on any day in this building's 40 year history.

Thanks to the increased staff and physicians who flew into action that day, the hospital never had to Divert. The term Divert, means hospital personnel notifies key state entities, such as Emergency Medical Services, to divert emergency patients elsewhere. If staffing levels are too limited to manage the depth of impending medical needs, diverting patients to other capable hospitals is always an option.

My car radio tuned to a local FM station and listening for any information about what happened at the parade, I headed to the hospital. There was no news being broadcast yet. As I pulled up to the driveway designated for off-site hospital employee parking off of Seventh Avenue, two of our facilities employees waved me past. I rolled down the window as one of them approached and said, "Scott, we're holding this area for helicopters. We need you to park over there." He pointed to the parking lot next door.

"Oh, absolutely!" I said.

Rolling up my window and backing away from that entrance, I thought "Okay...what the heck?" I turned my car around and pulled into the Career Tech state offices parking lot next door on the west side of the hospital. We have a helipad on the roof directly above the Emergency Department, but to hold that entire parking area indicated the potential magnitude of what we were about to encounter.

Placing a call to Foundation colleague, Jeffery Corbett, I said, "Have you heard anything about an event at the end of the homecoming parade?" Walking through the hospital parking lot, I cleared my throat as I saw a second helicopter fly overhead toward the crash site.

There are only ten air ambulance helicopters in the state of Oklahoma and on this day eight of them were in Stillwater, transporting patients from the site of impact. Some made multiple trips to and from Stillwater given the enormity of the calamity.

"I heard a couple of helicopters and figured they were news stations covering the parade," Jeffery said.

"A crash of some sort happened at the end of the parade. There are several people hurt and possibly even some dead. Can you meet me at the hospital?" I asked. "We might need to help with the media and visitors if you're available and up for it."

"Sure, I'll be right there," Jeffery said.

Though we had only worked together six months, I knew Jeffery would meet me at the hospital. Committed and detail oriented, Jeffery had been a loyal hospital employee for 22 years, and having him present would be enormously helpful.

From our earlier phone conversation, I couldn't grasp the depth of what Shyla said until I walked into the hospital fifteen minutes later. Fatalities and multiple injuries said it all. I went inside and observed many people standing and talking with one another, several obviously injured. No one in the waiting room was screaming, but some were crying still in shock and others were clearly in pain, the most seriously wounded were already being triaged.

Our ED waiting room which typically seats 30 people had folks sitting in almost every chair and a few even in wheelchairs. In the coming hour, people continued flowing in the doors of our ED waiting room.

I saw a gentleman standing at our ED desk calmly talking to our long-time, award-winning employee, Marie West. The man was Mark McNitt, an OSU alum from Houston, who happened to be in town for the game with his wife, Angela, and his parents, Sharon and Leo Schmitz.

I overheard Mark say, "My mom was on the bus." Still not knowing incident details, I thought maybe a bus was somehow involved in the barricade breach Shyla referenced. I only learned his name the next day, as I sat in my living room Sunday watching television, while he stood at the podium wearing the same OSU hat and sweatshirt he was wearing the morning of the crash.

Initially, I was tasked with helping ensure the media did not show up at the hospital and begin asking questions of victims and their families. Some members of the media have a reputation of being callous or focused on slanting a story for sensationalism. The last thing any of these victims or their families needed was to speak to media.

Fortunately, our state's media didn't show up at the hospital that morning, and they fully respected the request for them to gather downtown at City Hall. With our ED waiting room approaching near capacity, I helped by escorting those uninjured friends and family into our hospital's West Conference Room. This was a central place where families could wait for their loved one to be released or where other hospital officials could update them individually as more information became available.

Unfortunately, little information was coming from the crash site, and I was unable to answer the most basic questions; How many victims were still there? Where are other victims being sent?

With smartphones in hand, I believed our guests were likely getting more information via texts and phone updates from the back rooms of our hospital than I could provide. Given my role in the hospital and our strict adherence to health information privacy, I am never privy to patient health information unless a patient or family member shares something directly with me.

It was quiet in the West Conference Room. Though no one wanted to be there, it was certainly a more calming and comfortable atmosphere. As all hospital employees are trained, I addressed the group using "AIDET" and explained as more information was available we would share it with them.

Thanks to our hospital's Studer Consulting training, our approximately 1,300 Stillwater Medical personnel are each trained in AIDET, which stands for:

Acknowledge our guests by kindly welcoming them;

Introduce ourselves and our background or training experience;

Duration sharing how long we may be helping the patients or their families;

Explain to those patients, families, or guests to the best of our ability, so they know what to expect from their visit with us;

Thank them for coming to our hospital and expressing appreciation for them, while encouraging them to let us know how we might make their visit a positive experience.

In a normal patient visit situation, this can be calming or pleasing to a patient and their family as they learn about the situation, procedure or process they will encounter and what they may expect while they are with us. I could tell this group of 10 people were appreciative I had provided my AIDET introduction. However, because they were friends and family members for a larger group that had all arrived at the hospital with injured loved ones, they were not permitted to go into the ED because the emergency rooms are meant for only one or two other people in addition to the patient, doctor, and nurses.

As you might expect, the expressions on the faces looking back at me reflected deep sadness and concern, though they appreciated the fact that we were communicating with them. They knew we would do our best to keep them informed if there was anything about which to inform them.

Meanwhile, in the areas where patient care is typically provided, our hospital staff, including the aforementioned doctors, nurses, techs and assistants, were racing to assess traumatic injuries. They were working to save lives, just like they do each and every day. However, today they were just doing it with a more significant patient load than is typical.

As I returned to the main hallway just outside of the emergency room, I was thankful to see counseling staff from our university community already on hand to lend a shoulder or an ear. Though I personally wouldn't realize I needed counseling myself until later, I knew having Lee Bird's and Suzi Burk's counseling skills there was a godsend for the victims, their families, their friends, and our Stillwater Medical team.

The looks of shock and pain in the eyes and on the faces of those standing and sitting in the ED illustrated a hint of what must have engulfed the scene at that intersection. With no clear appreciation of what exactly transpired, from time to time I observed only the people arriving looking for loved ones, in a panic for what they might find.

Several blocks away from City Hall at Stillwater Medical Center, wearing a black and white dress, Shyla looked as though she may be stepping in front of the camera at any minute to convey the Stillwater Medical response to this major situation still unfolding.

"Shyla, I'm glad to do whatever I can to help. What do you need done?" I said.

"Thankfully Mayor Noble, President Hargis, the OSU Alumni Association, the Stillwater Police Department, and Stillwater Emergency Management called a news conference to be held at City Hall," Shyla said. "We are to direct media down there. If any media do show up here, tell them the press conference at City Hall is supposed to begin about 12:30 p.m. We need to do what we can to make the victims' family members comfortable while they are here and try to keep the waiting room clear."

PRESS CONFERENCE

Chris Batchelder flanked OSU President Burns Hargis, Mayor Gina Noble, and Stillwater Police Department Captain Kyle Gibbs in front of Stillwater City Hall as they articulated what "fouled" this special day. At the press conference, Batch was stunned at the level of detail the Stillwater Police Department had compiled relating to the facts of the case before the cameras were live.

Standing at that press conference, Batch became part of a national news story, the association's previous leaders could never fathom would occur. Captain Kyle Gibbs of the Stillwater Police Department was the initial spokesman describing the known facts.

Less than a year after he officially took on the role of new Services Bureau Captain and Public Information Officer for the Stillwater Police Department, he was standing at one of the most challenging podiums of his career to date. Stillwater leaders came together to answer questions, discuss briefly what had occurred at the end of the parade route, show support for the families, and discuss how the day would proceed as the hour for a nationally televised football game was approaching.

President Hargis has served in that capacity since 2008. As a successful attorney, a former Oklahoma A&M College Regent, and dutiful civic volunteer, he made a run for Oklahoma's Governor 20 years earlier and served as an articulate, quick-witted host on a weekly political television segment called "Flash Point." He well understood the pressures of standing behind a podium with media yearning for more detail in tough to answer questions. As usual, Hargis' words were spot on saying all that needed to be said on behalf of the University at that moment.

An educator in Strategic Communications at Oklahoma State University, Mayor Gina Noble had been our mayor for just under one year. She made brief, thoughtful remarks, expressing her heartfelt sentiments for the families of those killed and injured, while behind the scenes city staff and other officials were working to process the scene and re-open the intersection.

THE HARRISON FAMILY

Globally, Rotarians share friendships and the bond of the four-way test:

Is it the truth?
Is it fair for all concerned?
Will it build goodwill and better friendships?
Will it be beneficial to all concerned?

In the hallway at Stillwater Medical, I literally bumped into David Harrison, an acquaintance from my Stillwater Frontier Rotary Club whom I was just about to step around when he called my name.

"Scott, I need help finding my daughter, Kelly," David said.

Neither of us wore our typical weekday necktie, and we were out of context. A Rotary member less than a year, I looked into his eyes knowing I should know him, and he said. "It's Dave Harrison from Rotary." He could have added "dummy" after he said Rotary.

"Oh gosh, Dave, yes, I apologize I didn't recognize you. How may I help?" I said.

His expression of shock and anguish spoke volumes, displaying a sadness his speech couldn't articulate. "Both of my daughters have been injured in this, Scott. Kimberly is here and my wife Suzie is with her. Kelly was flown from the scene and is in critical condition, but no one can tell me where she was taken," David said.

"I'm so sorry. I'm confident we can find out where she is," I said.

He had already asked the question, but no one could tell him where she was sent because no one knew. Not the police, not the hospital, not the fire department, not LifeNet nor Stillwater Emergency Management knew where his daughter had been flown.

They tracked each patient being loaded into a helicopter, but the eight helicopters inbound and outbound complicated the process at the scene. A couple of the choppers were actually diverted to different hospitals once airborne. Nothing about the dispatching of patients from the scene was simple.

David's anxiety of not knowing where Kelly was flown or the severity of her condition only heightened his mounting trepidation. In all, thirteen patients were flown to other hospitals on those eight air ambulances.

We both imagined I could waltz into the back of the hospital and get in touch with someone who could provide answers. I just assumed I could easily help David find Kelly.

I started at the ED front desk to check with Marie. She knew nothing about victims transferred from the scene, but I did learn Kelly had not been brought to our hospital. I discovered that the more serious injuries were all being airlifted. That's when I learned that there were multiple helicopters flying patients to multiple Oklahoma City and Tulsa hospitals.

I told David what I learned. When I shared the unknown, his eyes pierced mine. It was as if I was reading his mind, and he wanted to shout, "What in the hell do you mean no one knows where my daughter was flown?"

Of course, David didn't say those words. Having two children of my own, I imagined my empty response left a frustrating void in his heart. From the continued uncertainty, like standing near a fire, I felt the intensity of his burden.

"I will keep asking questions. Do you want to have a seat in the West Conference Room rather than stand here in the hall?" I asked.

"I'll just wait here," he said.

I was on a mission. Looking for a staff member with a clipboard, grease board, computer monitor, a printed list, I was seeking any helpful thread of information about his daughter, Kelly.

No one had answers.

Literally every staff member was engaged in patient care on some level. Every room had a patient and every staff member, whether a doctor, nurse, or scrub tech, was focused and on task. This team is highly trained to care for patients in the worst imaginable condition, but as for a disaster, this Mass Casualty Incident was the ultimate test.

Our entire team was taking care of business. A nurse would walk out of one room, sliding the barn-style door shut, and soon a doctor would walk in to proceed with his or her work. Like a machine, this consummate band of brothers and sisters bobbed and weaved in an organized, diplomatic, and cooperative fashion.

A concentrated passion and resolute calm filled the air. No one was screaming, yelled, or threw things; everyone focused. No matter whom I asked, no one knew where Kelly Harrison had been flown.

My thoughts ricocheted as to the cause, seeing such pain throughout our ED. Perhaps the person driving had a health event or was texting and driving. This devastation was unconscionable. A plethora of thoughts raced through my mind as I saw people with all imaginable injuries being triaged and treated in various hospital rooms. I had to stay focused on my task for the Harrison family.

Being a relatively small community, I recognized David Duncan, an ununiformed Stillwater Police officer with a clipboard standing at the front of the ED behind the door. Since I invested most of my time traversing between the

ED waiting room, the West Conference Room, and the areas where our caring professionals were triaging patients, I imagined someone at our hospital had answers or knew who would. I personally hadn't observed or heard one single helicopter arrive or depart from our parking lot yet, but for all I knew, several could have come and gone during that time.

"Officer Duncan, I'm trying to help David Harrison find his daughter who was flown from the scene. His oldest daughter Kimberly is here, and Kelly, his younger daughter, was flown, but no one knows where. Can you help us find out where she was sent?" I paused to breathe.

He didn't recognize me, but since he had done public information for the police department several years ago, he was frequently quoted in the paper or on the news, so I knew him. He carefully sized me up trying to determine what business I had asking him about an injury victim.

Hospital employees are instructed to wear hospital badges one hundred percent of the time while in the hospital, but my badge was in my truck, parked in an OSU Posse Parking lot outside of the football stadium.

"Who are you with?" Officer Duncan politely asked.

Touching my upper chest area with my right hand near my collar showing where my hospital badge should be hung, I said, "I'm Scott Petty. My badge is in my truck. I'm the director of the hospital foundation, but I'm trying to help Mr. Harrison locate his daughter who was flown from the scene by helicopter. He's in the hallway if you'd like to speak with him."

Officer Duncan recognized Kelly's name and told me that serious cases were being flown to OU Medical or Mercy in Oklahoma City, but maybe St. John's in Tulsa. David was slowly pacing in the hallway outside of our ED. He trusted I would return to him with information about his daughter.

I circled through the ED waiting room once more, checking at the registration desk and the main ED nurse's desk in the back, seeking anyone who might know something more.

Stopping mid-circle in the back hallway, I was alone. My thoughts heavy with David's burden, the shock of seeing traumatized patients, and the uncertainly of the cause all nauseated me. Family and friends were strong for their loved ones, but I was unexpectedly overtaken by the intensity of my emotions.

The sting David and so many others were experiencing forced me to process this stress differently. I had to breathe and focus on what I could do.

Regardless of where she was flown, it would take approximately 20 minutes of flight time from Stillwater. It seemed as though I had already been walking around trying to find answers that long.

The fact that I was being very little help and absolutely no one could tell me for sure where this injured person was sent weighed on me. I had one task, and I was failing.

Knowing my friend was literally just around the corner, I gathered my composure and rejoined him in the hallway, "It sounds like most of the patients are being flown to OU Medical Center or Mercy in OKC, but I'd really like to confirm that for you before you head that way."

Marie, an employee at the switchboard and ED front desk for over 25 years was, as always, just as cool as a cucumber in this not so calm situation. Audible pages echoed from the overhead intercom for different names as hospital personnel tried to locate loved ones in other areas of the hospital. None of those pages called David's name.

My fellow Rotarian certainly didn't want to drive to Tulsa, 75 miles east, if his daughter had been flown 55 miles south to OKC. When law enforcement finally ascertained his daughter was headed to OKC, David left immediately, and I promised to phone him en route if I learned anything else.

Through this experience David and I fostered a bond that only comes through a shared pain, yet I felt only a fraction of his. I later visited both Kelly in Oklahoma City and Kimberly in our hospital, making sure they were progressing, expressing our sincere concern, and well wishes for their speedy recovery.

Though I worked in Physician Practice Management mostly in our SMC owned clinics for two years prior to accepting the SMC Foundation directorship, on this day, I observed things I had never seen in my professional life. I could not have been prouder of every single professional engaged in patient care that day and in the days to follow.

BHARDWAJ VARMA

Three friends of Bhardwaj Varma's arrived at the hospital and were asked to wait in the West Conference Room. Bhardwaj had been standing in the southwest corner of the intersection at Hall of Fame Avenue and Main Street. They walked into the conference room and it was at that time, I learned Bhardwaj's girlfriend was Nikita Nakal. Sadly, she was one of the victims that didn't survive the crash. One of the young men, also a student from another country emphatically said, "He mustn't call Nikita's parents to tell them of the incident. It is the middle of the night there now."

Bhardwaj's friends wanted to make sure he didn't call until a little later. After checking on his whereabouts in our hospital, I learned he was in the area where the walking wounded were being treated. So, explaining the importance of his privacy, I told them they would need to wait until he was released before they could see him. Offering to relay that message to him, I expected one of our nurses would likely deliver the message.

All of the nurses were caring for other patients at that moment, so I was directed to proceed into the very back of the area in which Bhardwaj was receiving care. Entering the doorway, I observed him in a conversation with a counselor and a nurse. Simultaneously, they looked into my eyes as I entered the doorway. Interrupting their conversation, I said, "Excuse me, Mr. Varma? You have some friends here and they will be waiting on you. They asked that you not call Nikita's parents yet since it is the middle of the night in India."

With a burdened expression of raw sadness, he slowly said, "Okay, tell them I will not call them yet."

I said, "I am very sorry, sir."

Retreating to the West Conference Room, I relayed to his friends that Bhardwaj understood their request and he would wait to phone Nikita's parents. I resumed offering my assistance where needed and helped a few more walking-wounded. There were still no solid answers about why this tragedy occurred, and at this point it did not matter to our medical team as they were consumed with patient care. All anyone knew was one car and one driver created this mass trauma and altered hundreds if not more than a thousand lives in a few tragic seconds of pandemonium.

BIGGER THAN THE GAME

Cowboy Head Football Coach, Mike Gundy, was going through his home game day ritual after driving to the Atherton Hotel on the OSU campus from his home on the south edge of Stillwater. The football team has three different routine packages on game days depending upon the time of kick-off.

Those involve a plan for an 11 a.m. game, one for an afternoon game, and one for an evening game. Each of those routines involve multiple team meetings, free time, chapel, a meal, and "The Walk." Like pieces of a puzzle each requires different timing depending upon the start time.

Given the scheduled 2:30 p.m. kickoff of the homecoming football game with the University of Kansas on October 24th, the players were preparing to have their pregame meal and the first of their team meetings in the Student Union. As Coach Gundy arrived for the first gathering of their morning, it was 11 a.m. He walked into the common area and immediately noticed his team of seventy dedicated athletes acting differently.

They are usually getting focused, listening to music, or casually visiting with one another. Gundy noticed they weren't being themselves. Instead of being embroiled in their own music, he noticed that they were huddled in groups, and literally everyone was looking at their telephones eyebrows raised and awestruck demeanors.

Through his 26 years in collegiate coaching, Gundy has become proficient in reading body language. When it comes to observing others, especially student-athletes, he skillfully reads non-verbal cues quickly sizing up circumstances. It makes him a great coach. He does it constantly, both on and off the field.

There has been considerable debate in coaching circles regarding whether it is wise to allow players to have their phones during game day prep. Given the various uses for these hand-held devices, the Cowboys are permitted to use their phones, like all college students use their phones, until it becomes time to place 100% focus on the game ahead. In Gundy's opinion, they are college students, and depriving them of the right to have a phone or music on game day could create distress among his players and coaches.

On game days, Coach Gundy's personal routine involves leaving his own cell phone in another room. His absolute and total focus is on the game and his players. He models and prefers no distractions, ignoring what's happening with other games, media, social media, texts, or anything not relating to OSU Football.

Aware of the mood in the room that morning, Gundy saw his Director of Football Operations, Mack Butler, walking briskly toward him. Mack coordinates transportation, hotels, meals, and security, and he assists in managing Gundy's obligations relating to public appearances and certain meetings. Normally a gregarious, friendly, and detail-oriented fellow, Mack typically has little interaction with Coach Gundy on game day. However, today his expression told Gundy he was about to hear something that he didn't want to hear.

"Something big just happened at the parade. There was some sort of an incident," Mack said.

"An incident, what kind of incident?" Gundy said.

"We don't know, but it isn't good. People are injured. I'll get more information to you as soon as I know more," Mack said.

Gundy made a coaching decision to withhold the minimal information they had from the team. Since they didn't have any facts yet, there was no reason to tell the team about the situation that they would shortly learn was no accident. Still observing his student-athletes with their phones in hand and their somberly huddled, group-like engagements, the team already had more information about the wreck than he did.

The coach overheard someone talking about a car driving into a crowd of people. Pondering the possibilities and considering terrorism, he just couldn't believe something so terrible may have hit Stillwater during the city's largest celebration of the year.

Key Oklahoma State figures in facilities management and university communications were in constant contact with each other. Assistant Director of Athletics Facilities, Marty Sargeant, OSU's Director of Communications, Gary Shutt, and OSU's Senior Vice President and General Counsel, Gary Clark, were all in close contact with Mack. Mack was in close contact with Gundy, so the chain of communication was as strong as possible.

Returning to Gundy later, Mack described the many injuries and deaths. Gundy's thoughts raced to his own family. Though their eldest son was out of state, Mike wasn't sure where his wife Kristen or their two younger boys were. Kristen and the boys were reached and were all safe.

Given that news, they took a collective sigh of relief, going on with their day's plans. Since no official call on the game had been made, they kept their routine schedule and started "The Walk." They decided they would proceed with their regular game plans until they heard the decision from Big XII Officials and Fox Broadcasting as to whether or not they were going to play the game.

"The Walk" is a home football tradition involving Cowboy Football loyalists, which began during Coach Gundy's days as the Associate Head Coach. This well coordinated two-block stroll takes place when all football players, coaches, the Cowboy Marching Band, and the OSU Spirit Squad walk through a parade-like gauntlet. It is a festive atmosphere, with music blaring and fans cheering.

Everyone nearby falls in, lining the curbs near Hester Street for this voyage from the Student Union to the west endzone entrance of Boone Pickens Stadium. Scores of fans, in some places stacked eight to ten people deep, stretch their necks to get a glimpse of their student-athlete friends, family members, or other notable players or coaches.

Coach Gundy recognized an absence of fans, the smallest crowd he'd ever witnessed at "The Walk." As always, the OSU Band, Spirit Squad, and Pistol Pete led "The Walk" down Hester Avenue.

The marching band played the fight song, Pistol Pete stood tall aboard his John Deere Gator waving to the crowd, signaling his trademark arm gesture spelling out OOOO-SSSS-UUUU. However, the very few people in attendance didn't possess their typical enthusiasm.

As a graduate of Oklahoma State, Gundy could only assume like one big family supporting each other, the normally giddy fans cheering with excitement were instead watching the news at their tailgates, huddled with friends trying to reconcile what had unfolded.

Once the team arrived at the stadium, Mack asked Gundy the question everyone had been thinking, "Do you think we should play the game?"

Without hesitation, Mike said, "This is way above my pay grade. With people losing family members, it's not my decision. We'll do whatever you tell me we need to do."

Ultimately, the decision to play the game was made. Before the start of the game, having now been provided factual information through the reliable university communications chain, Coach Gundy finally knew enough details to know the crash wasn't an act of terrorism. He also knew no other potentially threatening acts against fans or players were expected. He was ready to address his team.

Having faced adversity before, he implored his team play for the families who lost loved ones. He inspired them to do their best today, and then their efforts after the game would be to help the families and support the victims in any way they possibly could.

Collecting himself and now standing before his team and coaches, his mind filtered words and channeled emotions, Gundy said.

"You guys know something horrible happened at the homecoming parade today. These things happen in life and you'll be faced with events like this in your own life, and you'll have to deal with them to the best of your ability. As you mature, things may happen to your parents, your wife, or to your own children. You'll have to learn to accept them.

This is a terrible tragedy, and you'll have to learn from this situation and make the most of it. You may not understand it now, but it will make you a better person. This is bigger than any game. Today, out of respect for these families, you will play for people who have been affected by this. In a sense, you're playing for everybody in the country because now—their eyes are on you." Gesturing with his index finger to his players in a sweeping motion."

With that Gundy stopped speaking and looked into the eyes of his players, knowing the fewer the words the better. That was all they needed to hear.

The Cowboys prevailed over the Kansas Jayhawks with a lopsided 58-10 victory. With class and compassion, Coach Gundy shared in his postgame news conference, that he didn't have many details regarding the incident prior to the start of the game. However, he explained to his players and coaches that certain life occurrences are out of their control.

He again led his team by proclaiming "we can only control what we do," and in the days that followed, his team would do what they could to support the families of those injured and killed in this horrible crash. Multiple players visited crash victims at Stillwater Medical, in homes, and elsewhere on their own time and often with little fanfare because that was the right thing to do. It lifted the spirits of those who were healing and helped Cowboy football players understand the importance of their role.

Gundy has weathered some fairly ferocious storms with his players while becoming the winningest Cowboy football boss to date. I've known him fairly well for over 20 years, but with still an outsider perspective, I'll tell you, he models and strives doing it the right way.

He sees himself as a father figure to his players, partially because some of his athletes never had a father growing up. Some of his players never had a male role model holding them accountable, helping them set goals, and forcing high expectations.

Gundy commits to building good men first and foremost. He may be a very good coach, but he is an even better human being, inspiring the best from those who are chasing their academic and athletic dreams. Daily, Gundy instills a vital culture of compassion in his players, building character which will last them a lifetime.

GAME DAY: LAW ENFORCEMENT ROLES CONTINUE

Like many in the ranks of law enforcement on this day Officer Radley, Lt. Charles, and Lt. Chandler's responsibilities didn't end after the last injured patient was removed from the crash scene. Reporting to Boone Pickens Stadium to work the OSU vs Kansas football game, this was no ordinary day for them, their peers, or anyone in Stillwater for that matter. Unfortunately, for those protecting our families and other fans until the game's final gun, it set-up to be an extremely long day.

Typically scheduled to work four, ten-hour days per week, on any given day officials on the police force are exposed to hours longer than that. Sometimes our society's most challenging elements and sad images are unrelenting for those on patrol.

Officer Radley later heard rumors that he was on his cycle when it got hit. Some of those rumors were that he had actually died. Unintentionally fanned by emotion, rumors can burn into perceived reality through events like this. Later Officer Radley, his family, and their friends had sincere heart-to-heart conversations regarding how they should expect to hear from him or anyone else when the chips are down.

They now understand in a catastrophic incident like this he may only text, "I'm okay." He will call if he can, but if someone is standing at his family's doorstep then that is likely when the news is bad.

At one point during the game, while standing in the press box surveillance command center, Lt. Charles scanned the multiple closed-circuit TV monitors, one camera focused on the Hall of Fame and Main Street intersection. On that monitor, he could see the three deceased bodies still lying in the street and the handful of officials still diplomatically processing the scene.

Surreal beyond words to Lt. Charles, this major athletic event with 65,000 cheering fans was underway in spite of the tragedy down the street. Likely none of those fans knew halfway through the football game, victims were still laying in the intersection three blocks east.

In his mind, Lt. Charles compared the image to some war-torn city in the Middle East. He felt sick gazing at the crime scene with three dead bodies still respectfully draped awaiting the medical examiner's investigation.

The entire stadium reverently bowed in a moment of silence remembering those victims and their families. The fact that there are families just learning that their loved ones would never walk through their door again made zero sense.

Given today's undermanaged mental health concerns and the climate of political tension throughout the United States, Lt. Charles notes he and his law enforcement peers are well-trained and prepared to handle an active shooter and other difficult scenarios requiring armed force. However, except for table top trainings, preparation for a mass casualty incident where a car rams through a crowd of innocent bystanders at a high rate of speed is not something anyone expected to deal with in Stillwater. Ever.

"Today in the United States, it's clearly no longer 'IF' a situation might occur, but rather 'WHEN' a situation will occur." Lt. Charles said.

As a city under 60,000 residents, managing a single trauma event involving approximately fifty people at once became a test beyond expectations.

"I could not have been more proud of our officers and others rendering much needed and timely aid," Lt. Charles said.

STILLWATER EMERGENCY MANAGEMENT AGENCY

His right arm was struck by the driver-side mirror of the tan car that barreled through the intersection, creating so much human devastation. However, hours later Stillwater Emergency Management Volunteer, Todd Crosby, was still standing over one of the deceased adult victims at the intersection of Main Street and Hall of Fame. The shock and anger had not softened; Todd still grappled with what violated Stillwater. As the receding homecoming fans vacated the caution tape, turned crime tape draped four corners, and headed to the homecoming football game, the solitude of the intersection become the SEMA team's sanctuary.

As the game began, less than half a mile west of Main Street just beyond Duck Street, Todd heard the Oklahoma State University football fans roar in jubilation for a good play that occurred on the field.

"It felt so surreal that here was an appalling death. I'm standing over a lifeless woman and three blocks away football fans have no idea we are awaiting the medical examiner and crime investigators to finish processing the scene," Crosby said.

The intersection was cleared of each scrap of debris and restored to the original, pre-crash intersection. Following protocol, SEMA's Rob Hill asked each of his team members to check in with the folks present to help them address their mental health needs. His dedicated team, who had been through so much, were responsible for scheduling a time to meet with a counselor in the future. He then dismissed them so they could finally be with their families.

Though they did check in, not one of the SEMA team left at that time. They each wanted to ensure after the football game the fans driving through that intersection would not observe any sign of a catastrophic event just hours earlier. Not until after the street washer left, was the SEMA team's work complete.

Unfortunately, the parade traffic on those four corners and along those streets included approximately 1,000 adults and children who, if looking, may have had a clear vantage point at the moment of impact. The compassion and love those individuals provided instantly to strangers and loved ones would be the impetus for "Stillwater Strong" to come to life and strengthen our resolve around the world.

Stillwater Strong, the name propelled by social media within minutes of the crash, fostered community support and prayers for healing and strength. In the days that followed the tagline served as an inspiration for victims, volunteers, and first responders. It captured an infinite healing strength and became the deliberate cause created by the Stillwater Medical Foundation allowing philanthropic support from thousands who sought to help those injured and the families of those killed.

AFTER

Service Above Self

THE BATES FAMILY

Remarkably, Paul Bates learned his wife, Sheri, had no serious internal injuries. However, she had a broken left leg, some broken vertebrae, a fractured jaw, and a serious head injury including a crack in her skull radiating from the back to the front. Sunday morning doctors told Paul she now had an aneurysm in her brain and explained they would have to immediately do brain surgery to remove it.

To gain perspective regarding the seriousness of Sheri's head injury, imagine the equator circling the circumference of planet earth. Her head fracture extended nearly 180 degrees, from the center of the back of her head, through her right ear region, continuing to her nasal cavity stopping nearly at her nose. Though her seven or eight other serious physical injuries required months to heal, her devastating Traumatic Brain Injury (TBI) would be the most complicated of them all. A TBI of this magnitude requires months and sometimes years of therapy.

Thanks to social media and the lightning speed with which news circles our globe, Sheri Bates' family in Canada and Singapore learned about the tragedy almost instantaneously. Unbelievably, their relatives in those countries learned they had loved ones directly impacted and in a serious way. Almost immediately, friends from their church initiated and received prayers of healing and encouragement. In fact, prayers and support from countless countries around the world stretching from Ecuador to Italy, and India to Cambodia came through.

Charitable donations poured into multiple funds created for the family. Lakeside Bank, Sheri's employer, held a bake sale and created an account for customers and community members to support Sheri in her recovery and the avalanche of support was completely overwhelming. There were two GoFundMe pages set up for Sheri, so both Paul and her supervisor Jeremy assured her at her hospital bedside everything would be taken care of, so there was no reason to worry about finances.

Sheri has vague memories of the actual parade before impact and remembers very little about her first three weeks in the hospital at OU Medical Center. Prior to being injured, she didn't even know where the OU Medical Center was located.

#STILLWATERSTRONG

The morning after this unbelievable life event on Sunday, October 25, 2015, I slid out of bed and onto my living room couch about 4 a.m. After a practically sleepless night, I flipped on the news, and there it was, crawling on ESPN, CNN, and all of the major networks. However, still no concrete details answering why. I was drawn to help the victims I had seen in our hospital and the families who lost loved ones.

Like #BostonStong after the Boston Marathon bombing, #StillwaterStrong began trending on social media after this unsettling event unfolded that homecoming morning. My mind reeled all night about the victims and their families, whom I had seen in our hospital along with so many others hospitalized elsewhere. I felt called to do more.

While scrolling several social media sites, I kept noticing "go fund" accounts had been created. But by whom? Were these accounts legit or even approved by the families? Were these real people accepting donated funds that would ultimately get to the families of those injured or killed?

Were these authentic efforts to help those injured? The one thing I knew for certain, these types of funds were not permitting "charitable" or "tax deductible gifts" for donors to be directed to the victims and their families.

These described funds are received online by a "for profit" company, meaning the donor pays fees off-the-top to make the "gift." Did these families understand that or did they even know these funds were created? Could it be they didn't realize nearly 10% of their friends' donations went to a private, enterprising company providing that avenue to help? This company provided a brilliant, heart-felt technological option, powered by the vast networking promotions coming from social media, but a private entity makes money from it.

Anyone who knows about these various online fundraising efforts has also heard of the potentially fraudulent and deceitful efforts some people have portrayed in an effort to secure funds for people allegedly in need or in the name of individuals who truly are in need.

Before sunrise Sunday, I decided the Stillwater Medical Foundation would provide a legitimate and transparent opportunity for friends, families, alumni, and donors to support these families in their desperate time of need. I knew the Cowboy faithful and the state of Oklahoma would want to support these victims and their families. I felt it was our duty to accept charitable gifts to help. I didn't know at the time that our effort would stretch from coast-to-coast, then, ultimately wrap around the world from India to China to Columbia.

From everyone who has been given much, much will be demanded;
and from the one who has been entrusted with much,
much more will be asked.

LUKE 12:48   (NIV)

By Sunday afternoon, the Stillwater Medical Foundation activated a donation portal on our website, creating the Stillwater Strong Fund. Our team only did this for the victims and their families, whom we validated through law enforcement, court records, or other reasonable means. We created the fund in hopes of making some small difference and possibly, helping victims recover or rebuild their lives. Our mission was to make a difference in every physically impacted life. From day one we decided the Stillwater Medical Foundation would not take one cent for expenses to administer this fund.

Our original vision was to assist in easing the pain of loss for the surviving families of the four victims who perished as well as those injured in some manner. On that Sunday morning, I didn't know if we could discount medical bills. I didn't know if we could adequately assist in paying victims' bills. Having never embarked upon this type of endeavor, I didn't know if we would raise even $50,000 or $100,000. I simply concluded we would step forward and try to help.

Given the circumstances of the air ambulance flights and the numbers we had seen at our hospital, I expected the bills for those injured and killed could be staggering. I only hoped victims wouldn't be disappointed with what level of support we would provide.

At the time we initiated the fund, no one knew that Stillwater Medical would make a surprising announcement in the weeks ahead about the hospital bills for the injured victims who were seen at our hospital. For those victims and their families, the week of Thanksgiving brought much for which to be thankful. Stillwater Medical Center administration acted independently from the Stillwater Medical Foundation and announced they would not send a single victim a bill for their care at SMC that day or during their stay for those who had to stay multiple days for recovery following surgery. That action was a generous six-figure gift to victims and their families that no one expected.

The day after the crash, Mark McNitt found himself in a press conference standing next to his Mom and behind multiple microphones. In front of clicking cameras at the OU Health Center, he attempted to compose himself. Speaking extemporaneously, Mark described the gush of wind and the scary scene that followed.

He also addressed the condition of his stepdad, Leo Schmitz. There was a strong chance Leo may not wake up from his coma or survive his injuries. With confidence and grace Mark expressed the family's genuine appreciation for the prayers and countless public and private gestures of kindness. It was the beginning of a long and winding road for their family and many others.

OSU Alumnus Mark McNitt at the press conference at OU Medical Center in Oklahoma City.

FOR PETE'S SAKE

The day after the crash, Taylor Collins began receiving calls from media outlets seeking interviews to ask him about his involvement after the crash. Would his actions have made an impact in the media if he wasn't the university's mascot? Most likely not. Others had far more heroic acts given their skills and proximity to the crash. Stories propelled and shared through Facebook circulated about various people who were near the crash site and those aiding others when they needed it most.

Though Taylor had done a couple of newspaper interviews after being selected as Pistol Pete, the idea of being in front of a TV camera to talk about what he did as a private citizen seemed inappropriate, given the fact that four lives were lost. Talking about what he had done didn't seem right, so Taylor decided to call the OSU Alumni Association and spoke to Chris Batchelder.

Knowing the news media would be swarming campus and the OSU Alumni Association building two days post-crash, the OSUAA wanted to be consistent about managing the possible influx of media requests. The administrative team instructed staff on what to say and how to handle the homecoming crash topic should they be approached by media.

Batch asked a staff member to take Taylor across campus to meet with OSU's Director of Communications, Gary Shutt. Together they discussed best practices in doing TV and print media interviews. Gary provided Taylor some useful tips ensuring he adequately and appropriately answered media questions and if the requests kept coming and became overwhelming he could refer them to Gary.

Multiple times over the next few days Taylor spoke into a microphone held in front of his chest by a reporter and he answered the same questions.

"Where were you when the crash occurred?"

"Could you describe what you witnessed at the scene?"

"What did you do?"

"Why did you leap into action?"

"How does it make you feel to know you helped the victims you transported?"

"Would you do it again?"

With every question, Taylor answered thoughtfully and genuinely. He understood the appeal of a key university figure being involved, so he grasped why he advanced as part of the story and the media knew viewers wanted to hear something positive about events following the crash.

Courtesy of OSU Alumni Association

OSU mascot Pistol Pete, Taylor Collins, drove two crash victims to Stillwater Medical in his pick-up minutes after the crash. Many students were in the right place at the right time lending assistance, and Taylor's was one story that received national attention.

THE LANE FAMILY

The first person to contact me Sunday after learning the Stillwater Medical Foundation planned to create a charitable fund to assist victims and victims' families was a student named Jacquelyn Lane. She was a Junior majoring in Chemical Engineering from Beulah, Colorado, serving as a student senator with OSU's Student Government Association (SGA).

She had carried the lead banner for the OSU Homecoming parade – her trauma surgeon father Dr. Gary Lane, and her youngest sister Kaitlyn, assisted on the scene standing within feet of the crash when it occurred. Growing up the child of a physician, Jacquelyn was peripherally inspired by her father's passion of caring for and serving others.

I met Jacquelyn two days after the crash and was immediately impressed with her articulate confidence. Her genuine smile and heartfelt enthusiasm for the victims' needs led me to believe she could rally campus troops, including students, administration, faculty, alumni, and friends.

Jacquelyn had already reached out to Dr. Lee Bird, the Vice President of Student Affairs, who oversees the student clubs on campus and had also previously served as chairperson of our Stillwater Medical Foundation board of directors. Dr. Bird also supervises university counseling services and knows the OSU student body as well as anyone on campus.

In her tenure, Dr. Bird supported students and staff in the wake of the two latest OSU plane crashes, helping plan large campus memorial gatherings after those crashes. Now, she was planning another. Dr. Bird lost a close cousin in Tower II of the World Trade Center, so she has dealt with the aftermath of public catastrophic events on a personal and public level.

She and her staff were present in the halls of Stillwater Medical Center moments after the tragic homecoming parade crash, helping to meet counseling needs. Ultimately, Dr. Bird served on our Foundation's Stillwater Strong Committee helping to guide decisions about how to best assist the victims.

In addition to the Office of Student Affairs, Jacquelyn also reached out to the Student Government Association, OSU Foundation, the OSU Alumni Association, and Stillwater Medical Center administration. Jacquelyn's vision was clear. Create and sell t-shirts the profit goes to victims.

Each of those entities agreed to donate as well as help fund the purchase of the initial t-shirts to reduce the upfront costs. Each entity donated between $1,000 - $2,000 to secure the t-shirts. She needed to determine who would design, print, market, and sell them for the student body.

Jacquelyn's friend and fellow engineering student, Brandon Holle, inspired her to pursue the t-shirt idea. Brandon, the silent mastermind, guided her when she missed a class for a t-shirt meeting or needed test prep mentoring. All the while, Jacquelyn was in the midst of a grueling 19-hour academic load of a chemical engineering program.

Through our initial conversation, I believed in Jacquelyn enough to reach out to a dear friend who has sold millions of t-shirts from Stillwater, Oklahoma, since he founded his business in 1975. Jacquelyn and her SGA colleague, Jeremiah Taylor, sat down with me to review their concept of a t-shirt that they were confident OSU students would buy.

"Scott, students don't have a lot of money to donate, but we'll always buy a smart t-shirt design for a good cause, and I firmly believe we can sell some cool t-shirts," Jacquelyn said.

As a member of the millennial generation, she knew students are about purchasing a product for a cause.

"We're not really at that age where we can just donate money. We want something in return for our donation. That's why socially responsible companies are such a big hit with my generation," she said.

It was a certainly noble idea, but I also knew the team of two in our office would be crazy to tackle a vision like creating, marketing, and selling a Stillwater Strong shirt from our small foundation office. Our priorities are raising money for hospital needs.

However, Jacquelyn was so proactive before we met that she had already contacted two local t-shirt printers and learned they wanted money up front for the purchasing, creation, and printing of the shirt. No one wanted to outlay capital to sell shirts as a fundraiser. These obstacles didn't stop her.

"We got this!" Jacquelyn said with confidence. Given the correct contacts, I felt encouraged she could launch her dream to success.

STAN CLARK

His cell phone rang once, "Hey friend, how are ya?" the sincerity of the ever-smooth, voice said on the other end.

"I'm well, Stan. Thanks. Hey, do you have some time available in the next day or two? I need what may be a pretty big favor. Can we meet to talk about it?"

"Anything for you, pal. What's good?" Stan asked.

"How does tomorrow at 10 a.m. work? I've got a couple of students with a big idea, and we need to brainstorm," I said.

"See you then. Just come up to my office," Stan said.

That was it! Stan Clark, the visionary creator and founder of Eskimo Joe's, with the largest private brand of T-shirts in the state of Oklahoma and at one time the third most collectable t-shirt in the world, had given us the ultimate orange thumbs-up. Well, almost.

A day later, Jacquelyn, Jeremiah, and I scaled the creaking stairway of the historic Swim family home settling into Stan's second floor conference room. The former Swim home houses the iconic, Eskimo Joe's World Headquarters offices on Elm across from Stillwater's Jumpin' Little Juke Joint. Stan quickly made it clear for the student's benefit that he doesn't often open up to conversations with just anyone dreaming up a t-shirt idea.

Thankfully for all of us, I have known Stan well for many years, and he trusted me and my intentions and the invitation to help others in a time of need.

As we sat down, Jacquelyn exuded her youthful confidence. Stan asked questions about details and after almost an hour Stan said, "If we do this, I want to be clear; I want nothing in return. We'll seek no publicity. I'm only doing this because helping the victims is the right thing to do and because Scott asked me to meet with you." Stan paused, filling the room with a heavy sense of mounting expectation.

"I'm in!" He said.

Jacquelyn and Jeremiah floated down Joe's World Headquarters stairs as if it were a jet-powered escalator. They were on cloud nine--ty! Stunned by his frankness and swift conclusion, Jacquelyn admitted she nearly blurted out, "Come again?"

We knew there were no guarantees for success. But with the power of the Stan Clark Companies and the support of the University and the Hospital for these first few thousand shirts, we believed the students selling them through social media could fuel a frenzy.

They couldn't believe Stan said yes to their idea. Eskimo Joe's Promotional Products Group had the online presence and the back-office support to manage the expected sales volume. Stan's organization provided the brand status and a platform to supply the maximum return possible to the victims.

The students and Stan's creative leadership put their heads together on a design. Within days of the tragedy we had a design, and within another week we had thousands of t-shirts printed. Joe's Clothes had already promoted it online and pre-sold thousands to the Cowboy loyal. Committed students and citizens lined up to buy not just a t-shirt, but a good deed. People wanted to help, and the t-shirt provided the opportunity.

The official Stillwater Strong t-shirt created, marketed, and sold by both the OSU Students and Eskimo Joe's Promotional Products, directed 100% of the profits to the victims. Social media fueled the sale of 10,000 units in eight weeks.

The process and creation wasn't simple: there were significant debates about shirt fabrics, colors, styles, logos, etc., but the students felt they knew what would sell. They were focused, they were passionate, and they were right.

In the meantime, about five other Stillwater Strong t-shirt designs by private individuals popped up online. In those first few weeks, only two of those creators proactively contacted the Foundation to tell us of their plans. People have every right to do what they want. However, if they were promoting their shirts as though the funds were going to all victims through us, if they hadn't contacted us regarding their intentions, our Foundation couldn't endorse their product. If they told us they were directing their sale proceeds to the Stillwater Medical Foundation for the Stillwater Strong Fund we gladly added them to our list.

We did our best to validate those who were managing other t-shirt efforts. Verifying legitimate t-shirt designs benefitting Stillwater Strong victims was a process of following up and trusting people to honor their word.

We were grateful for the groups that contacted us early asking if they could provide their proceeds and present us with a donation. As we learned of others, we began contacting those people to find out what their intentions were and if they were donating directly to a friend who was injured or if they were directing their funds to our efforts.

Jacquelyn wondered how these other designs would impact the "Official" Stillwater Strong t-shirt promoted by the SGA, who had worked so hard to make their shirt concept legit by contacting us first. Anyone can design and sell t-shirts these days, so how easy would it be for someone to falsely say they were supporting the Stillwater Strong effort to support all?

Eventually, each of the shirt creators reached out to the Foundation as the buzz strengthened throughout television, radio, print, and social media.

Daily, we were contacted to track a new fundraising idea. For example, multiple retail stores wished to provide a percentage of profits from sales to our efforts. We did our best to validate and organize all requests, and we tracked at least sixty unique fundraising ideas from every angle.

Too late in the process, I received a call from a prison inmate telling us he designed a painting that he wanted us to auction to help the injured victims. Unfortunately, that inquiry came after funds had already been distributed and the Stillwater Strong Committee decided we wouldn't continue accepting funds after a certain date. So as one might imagine, the ripple effect of this tragedy grew sizably and the generosity was flattering.

I humbly sought Stan's permission to tell this story since, in the beginning, he emphatically requested they receive no publicity from their involvement in this effort. He graciously agreed for several reasons.

First, because as one of Stillwater's largest student employers, he understood the impact the Oklahoma State University student body had on the outcome of the t-shirt sales. Next, he completely grasped it was their contributions, passion, and drive that elevated the effort from creative concept to success, then to significance in less than two months.

Finally, Stan believes in and invests much in Stillwater and the University. Therefore, the opportunity for his team to join us in honoring those four lives lost, as well as the selfless community servants who stepped forward that day to aid them, has been beyond meaningful to his organization.

GARY SPARKS

I first came to know Gary Sparks at the time of the dedication of the OSU Plane Crash Memorial in Colorado in August of 2001. As a child he grew up moving from town to town across the United States as his dad worked in construction. From his early experiences, Gary learned the importance of sticking to something and building relationships for the long term.

Gary studied architecture at OSU in the early 1960s and met the love of his life, Jerri. To make money during college, he worked as the janitor at the United Methodist Wesley Foundation situated just south of campus on the north end of "The Strip."

Gary and Jerri's first date would be to an Oklahoma State basketball game in Gallagher Hall. In the late 1990s, Gary would ultimately dream up, on a napkin, how that historic Hall could be expanded from 6,381 seats surrounding the court's original white maple floor, to 13,611, on the same footprint where it has stood since 1938.

He shared the idea with then Director of Athletics, Terry Don Phillips. Gary thinks out of the box, and his creativity conceived the building we proudly hail as "the rowdiest arena in the country."

Gary called the Foundation three days after the crash and said, "Scott, I realize there probably isn't time to discuss this, but if you decide a memorial should be constructed to honor those lives lost, the surviving victims, and first responders, I'll donate my services to design a memorial concept."

Caught off guard by his offer, I said, "Gary, words won't express how much that would mean to our community. Thank you for that thoughtful invitation. If you have thoughts absolutely put them down. When the time is right, we'll get together with City and OSU officials to discuss."

I thought there would be a time and a place for such a tribute and also knew it was beyond my scope to accept that offer without speaking to City leaders, not to mention the families of the victims. So many kind offers were coming left and right, and I knew his inquiry was genuine. Since Gary designed the memorials in Stillwater and Colorado to honor the ten who lost their lives in the Colorado crash, he understood the importance of respecting and honoring those families so deeply impacted.

Gary designed a conceptual rendering of the memorial that included a solid base, featuring four panels with a small tribute to each of the four victims who perished. The concept displayed a tall alloy ribbon mounted atop the base surrounded by park benches for reflection. He engineered the memorial at an angle in which annually, on October 24th at 10:30 a.m., the sun's position will cast an encompassing shadow near the center of the memorial highlighting a key element of the memorial inside the neck of the ribbon.

Over the course of several conversations about materials and concepts, Gary and I met at Strickland Park, just east across the street from Hastings with a view of the crash site. The City already owned the property, and we took some photos of the landscape from different directions.

At that time, we didn't realize the City of Stillwater owned another small parcel of property directly northwest of the crash site, the perfect spot ultimately designated by the City as the location for the memorial site. The week of the 2016 OSU Homecoming a sign was erected near the site promoting the fact that this would be the future site of the memorial.

Now it would just be a matter of time for someone to pick up the ball and run with it. My hospital role focuses on Stillwater Medical priorities: the medical structures, medical equipment, or better experiences for our patients, physicians, and employees. This truly was on the fringe of where I needed to invest time. However, I believed many individuals and businesses would have an interest in supporting the concept, so in my spare time, I engaged community members in conversations sharing the vision of the memorial.

ANONYMOUS DONOR CHALLENGE

Several days after the crash and as would be the case in many of the days to come leading up to the self-imposed December 31st fundraising deadline, we received an inquiry from an individual who wished to make a donation to the Stillwater Strong effort. It had been a busy few weeks with lots of inquiries about our plans for funds, and multiple new charitable efforts continued popping up. Our office coordinator, Jeffery, and I were managing the various requests to authenticate to the best of our ability their legitimacy. This prospective anonymous donor was someone with whom I had interacted in the past, and whom had already supported the Stillwater Medical Foundation.

Wishing to remain anonymous, I assured him we would honor his request to the letter. The donor has since given me permission to share elements of this story to inspire others to give to causes important to them and to even give anonymously if that better suits the donor's needs.

This prospective donor was an OSU graduate who had been rocked by a life-threatening illness. In the wake of the OSU Homecoming tragedy, he watched from another state as players from the NBA's Oklahoma City Thunder basketball team and the OSU Cowboy Football team visited the surviving victims. He quietly cheered as victims made national headlines with their recoveries. The alum was moved by the actions of both the players and the medical community in Stillwater.

Cowboy Football players, (L to R) David Glidden and Mason Rudolph visit Stillwater Medical visiting patients and thanking staff and volunteers, (L to R) Dorothy Akin and Marilyn Filonow, for their service.

During our conversations, the donor reflected back to a day when the Stillwater Medical community rallied behind him in his personal recovery. Because of that, he and his family wanted to give back.

Twenty days after the crash, the donor told me that he would like to make a $10,000 donation. I was beyond elated by the family's generosity and knew this would be a great shot in the arm for the victims. Funerals, air ambulance transfers, and stout medical bills the living victims were facing could be financially devastating.

After thanking him profusely for his family's unexpected generosity and expressing our sincere appreciation, which I knew each victim of this crime would feel, I hung up the phone and walked into Jeffery's office to share the news of our largest donation to date. We could not believe the broad scale impact this cause seemed to be having in a few short weeks.

We witnessed a surge in donations and had increased requests from businesses and individuals to help raise money for the victims. We recruited hospital volunteers and Jeffery's wife, Annette, to help prepare donor receipts, address hand written thank you notes, and stick stamps.

We tried to keep this effort personal, meaningful and sincere. Several days following that gift being deposited, we received an unexpected call from the same donor.

His family had been thinking about the rippling impact of their contribution, and they wanted to offer a challenge option if we were willing to accept. The SMC Administration strongly discouraged us from asking anyone for major gifts, but rather only offer a trusting, transparent method for people to give. Hospital leadership also wanted the effort to end soon.

The donor and his family had done something similar during the relief effort following a devastating hurricane. They wished to offer a match if we could raise a certain amount.

"Scott, here's what we'd like to do," he said. "We'll match two to one every gift you receive between now and December 31st of this year up to $20,000. That means if you can raise $20,000 more, I'll give you another $40,000."

I was at a complete loss for words. From the beginning of the Stillwater Strong drive, I wondered if we could even raise $50,000. Now, thanks to the $10,000 this family had already given, they were offering to add up to another $40,000 more. Their gesture of confidence warmed my heart.

Overjoyed and at the same time highly challenged, I wondered if it was even possible for us to consider raising $20,000 more since our hospital administration specifically asked me to not solicit anyone for major gifts for this cause. To that point, we had only raised around $12,000 total. We had not yet defined exactly how these funds would be distributed, but I knew in my heart we were doing the right thing, even if we did only raise $50,000-$60,000.

Helping secure millions of dollars for major projects while working at the University Foundation was one thing. That typically happened following several meetings, often one-on-one and sometimes with a group, discussing intimate project details. We were just a small, local medical foundation launching into a significant undertaking to help OSU friends we had only recently, or not even yet met.

In our line of work, it is not typical of a traditional major gift donation to come via this method of giving, from someone with whom you barely know. Now an incredibly generous family offered to make their gift a $50,000 donation.

"SO! Guess what our anonymous donor would like to do now?" I asked Jeffery, describing our conversation details.

"So how do you suppose we'll get that $20,000?" he said, responding in a rather matter-of-fact, stone-faced demeanor and tone.

"I'm confident we'll get there, Jeffery. I'm confident we will." I said.

We honestly had no idea how many t-shirts would be sold through the SGA t-shirt effort, or how much other fundraising efforts might secure. However, I knew this: People wanted to help, and they liked knowing 100% of their donation would go to the families needing it most.

BEDLAM BUCKETS OF BLESSINGS

Twenty-five days after the crash, I received a call from long-time friend and a former OSU colleague Larry Reece. As public address announcer for our basketball and football teams, Larry's familiar baritone voice and an unrehearsed, effervescent personality engage everyone he meets. Spurred into a frenzy following a touchdown and the extra point kick, Cowboy Football fans erupt when the Voice of the Cowboys announces, "HERE COMES BULLET." Our galloping, black American quarter horse gelding then kicks into a sprint across the field with Oklahoma State's "Spirit Rider," making a u-turn at the thirty-yard line, proudly pumping the orange OSU flag.

Larry explained the OSU Athletic Department and OSU President's Office decided they would like the Stillwater Medical Foundation to pass buckets at the upcoming Bedlam football game between Oklahoma State and Oklahoma so our loyal and true alumni and Cowboy Football fans could donate to the victims. We didn't request this generous gesture; Larry's team at OSU believed this act would serve the victims and families in need.

Just a little over one week remained before the big Bedlam game against the Oklahoma Sooners. It's always a guaranteed capacity crowd regardless of the favored team. Our medical foundation had already been maxed beyond measure to keep up with the enormous volume of accepting donations, sending nearly one thousand receipts, writing thank you notes, tracking new fund raiser ideas, attending public events, and managing requests for assistance. Not to mention we were engrossed in developing a solid strategy for the timely and methodical distribution of these funds to the victims.

During the call I said, "Man, Larry, I'm completely flattered and just in awe of this offer, but I'm not sure we can make that happen. I mean, orchestrating the sheer magnitude and security required to handle the passing of the buckets during the Bedlam football game? I'm not sure we can pull that off."

This was a huge opportunity to gain awareness for our effort to help the victims through Stillwater Strong, but honestly, we couldn't do it alone.

The tradition of passing the bucket started at Oklahoma State when All American OSU wrestler, Ray Murphy, was paralyzed while wrestling for the Cowboys in 1970. This helpful bucket brigade concept had become an annual tradition and a way for the Cowboy family to show love and compassion for the Ray Murphy family and help with his steep medical bills until his passing in 2010.

I first witnessed a bucket being passed at an OSU Football game as a young boy in the late 1970's. Members of the OSU Cowboy Marching Band passed the sealed plastic buckets down rows and rows of the Lewis Field bleachers collecting donations from fans. Dad pulled out his wallet and pushed some bills through the small slot.

"We will help make it happen. OSU wants to do this for the victims and their families," Larry said.

Instantly, goosebumps rolled across my skin and a lump shot into my throat. I realized we needed to do it, and I trusted Larry. However, I grappled for several seconds over the sheer enormity of pulling it off without the experienced members of our Cowboy Marching Band. I paused as my mind raced through the process of checking approval boxes of what acceptance meant.

"Alright Larry, let's do it...I'm in," I said.

"Alright! Go Pokes, brother, Go Pokes!" Larry said.

"Go Pokes, brother!" I said back. "Go Pokes!"

HAWTHORNE ELEMENTARY'S BEDLAM INVITATION

The excitement of our state's Bedlam football game typically carries with it friendly jabs between fans and the opportunity for another year of bragging rights between Oklahoma State and the University of Oklahoma. The week before the football rivalry unfolded on the field, I participated in one of the most friendly and moving Bedlam experiences I've ever had; and I have had several since my days as an OSU student.

Thirty days after the crash, I visited Hawthorne Elementary School in Oklahoma City. Ms. Amanda Sloan received school administration approval to initiate a coin drive on our behalf of Stillwater Strong.

She indicated quite honestly, that their school wasn't in a wealthy neighborhood. Ms. Sloan shared that the students and teachers wanted to do something to make a difference and the lesson to help others in need was clearly an educational opportunity through which they wanted to inspire their students.

Knowing a little about this area, I perceived most of the students who attended this school were from middle-class and perhaps even lower income families. It warmed my heart knowing these children and this school were inspired to give to people they had never met. The profound lesson about helping others in their time of need made this school special.

Though coin drives don't typically raise significant amounts of money, the heart behind this gift was richly fulfilling because giving may have been difficult. They invited me to attend an assembly, and I felt it important to personally express my appreciation for their thoughtfulness and generosity.

The students wanted to present our Foundation with a check supporting Stillwater Strong and snap a photo. As it turned out, a couple of local television stations and a reporter from the Daily Oklahoman were there with a photographer to capture the check presentation and ask questions. They wanted to know what inspired the kids to give to this coin drive. From my angle, they wanted to understand more about whom we were helping, what we expected to do with these funds, and how soon we would be distributing the money.

As the students settled down, directly in front of me a cute, red-headed little boy caught my attention as he plopped into place criss-cross, apple sauce. Thoughts of Nash Lucas, the youngest crash victim, flooded my heart.

At the well-orchestrated school assembly, the teachers talked about how students and faculty wanted to help. The students read a poem about the importance of caring and giving before presenting the check to the foundation. It was a powerful statement, humbling to digest.

Tears of gratefulness and sadness bulged at the bottom of each of my eyelids, waiting to streak down my cheeks. As a different student read each powerfully poetic line, it seemed like a symphony's building crescendo swallowed the entire room hushed in silence.

The poem read aloud by these sweet voices said:

> *"Make a difference each day you live, open your heart, learn to give.*
>
> *Life for many is so unkind, giving people are hard to find.*
>
> *So open your heart, give what you can, we're all responsible for our fellow man.*
>
> *It's easy to look the other way, but the tables can turn on any given day.*
>
> *So help if you can for one day you may be the one who is down and out, the one no one will see."*

Those words captured the essence of what these kids gave and how this school modeled "paying-it-forward."

The students had been issued a challenge. If they secured $1,000.00 in coins to donate, the students would get to duct tape their assistant principal to the wall...and nearly $1,200.00 later, that is just what they did.

Children at Hawthorne Elementary School in Oklahoma City eagerly watch while Mrs. Cudd, standing on a chair, is willingly duct-taped to the wall.

The assembly participants watched, laughed, and cheered as fifty students took turns retrieving long strands of orange and black duct tape. The elementary kids hopped up on a chair and taped their assistant principal, Mrs. Cudd, to the wall. The school principal presiding over Mrs. Cudd's wall-taping, stood next to the chair ensuring the tape anchored well affixed to the wall.

I was pretty impressed when they removed the chair from underneath Mrs. Cudd, and there she stayed, stubbornly stuck to the wall like bubblegum to the sole of a shoe. Everyone cheered and some of the kids squealed from the top of their lungs with glee when Mrs. Cudd did the "running man" while stuck to the wall with orange and black duct tape, covering her Sooner pullover.

The school learned about setting and accomplishing a worthy goal, and they learned teamwork. Similar to our hospital's team effort to care for those victims in need that tragic October day, or the first responders that bolted into action at the crash site, multiple hands were required to attain the needed outcome. At Hawthorne Elementary the students' goals leading up to the event were exceeded. At the heart of it all was the passion to make a difference in the lives of those in need.

I climbed into my truck and tucked this meaningful $1,189.00 check into a deposit envelope and headed back to Stillwater. As I drove North on I-35, I couldn't help but reflect on this very brief, but truly impactful life of little Nash Lucas. He was only 2-years-old when he was tragically killed. Sadly, he would never spend even a day in an elementary school classroom as a student.

However, that day the lesson of Nash's young life and the impact he had on those students was monumental. I believe they understood the key to life is giving back, paying-it-forward and learning to help others. Those students keenly grasped that concept thanks to the teachers and administrators at Hawthorne Elementary School.

THE @RICKIEFOWLER EFFECT

Allen Adams of Pembroke, Massachusetts, a 1991 graduate from Oklahoma State University, was approaching the Hastings parking lot when he became aware of the chaos at the Main and Hall of Fame intersection. He was meeting the family of a student recipient of the scholarship honoring Allen's mother's memory.

His close proximity to the crash site lit up his voicemail as friends and employees back in Massachusetts contacted him asking if he was okay. Allen was fine, but emotionally he had changed.

When he returned he shared this change with his employees in Massachusetts, who then decided they wanted to do something to help. Only a few days after the crash, Allen contacted the Stillwater Medical Foundation asking if the Stillwater Strong effort could use a specially branded lapel pin.

Allen, the owner of All American Pewter, creates an array of innovative products. I welcomed this idea, and he offered to send me a few prototypes with different finishes to compare and decide if we wanted some for distribution. I wasn't sure how many we would need to buy, but I liked the idea of providing a gift to donors and giving a few to the victims, their families, doctors, and friends who helped on that tragic day.

When we agreed on a pin design, I reconnected with Allen.

"Thanks again for offering to create this lapel pin. How much would it cost for us to get 250-500 of them?" I said.

"Do you think that's that all you'll need?" he said. Cautious to not spend too much money that wasn't budgeted, I was guarded about buying too many.

"Well, we probably could use 1,000 if I could circulate them to the local banks and have them sell them or buy them for their customers, but I'd like to know what the price per pin might be before I commit," I said.

"You've got it. I'll donate them and I'll get the first shipment of 250 pins in the mail this week. You'll have another 500 as soon as I can make them," Allen said.

"Thank you so much! I'm not sure just thank you is substantial enough. Please know you and your team are truly appreciated and this will be meaningful to so many!" I said.

Once again, our Cowboy Family embraced our efforts with bold and unexpected acts of philanthropy.

Stylish PGA professional and former OSU Cowboy Golfer, Rickie Fowler was the "Guest Picker" on Game Day when ESPN came to the OSU campus less than one month after our homecoming celebration was tarnished. Rickie was one of those dignitaries that wore Allen's lapel pin on ESPN's Game Day in advance of our Bedlam game with OU. I knew if the pins were handy a true Cowboy fan would proudly pop it on to honor victims.

Rickie, one of Oklahoma State's most prominent ambassadors of orange, poked one of the pewter pins into his OSU hat. Capturing a shot of Rickie wearing it on the ESPN set in front of the OSU Library, I fired the picture to Allen moments later. He was elated beyond words that his creation and Stillwater Strong received some positive "Game Day" publicity.

Rickie Fowler appears on the set for ESPN Game Day sporting a Stillwater Strong pin donated by Allen Adams - All American Pewter.

Frankly, Rickie's All-American image, hometown favorite status, and his swiftly growing 1.5 million followers on Twitter didn't hurt our cause much either.

Nearly sixty individual and corporate efforts collaborated to make a difference. Those included multiple t-shirt sales, cell phone "Text to Give" campaign, 5K races, charity dinners and auctions and multiple silicone bracelet designs. Even specialized jewelry was created to honor victims. Several local restaurants and businesses provided a percentage of sales. Stillwater Strong auto stickers and even donations from a few dedicated OSU pregame tailgating collection jars provided a shot in the arm to the Stillwater Strong Fund.

We had generous support from our local Masonic Lodge, Young Professionals of Stillwater, and businesses such as Stillwater based InterWorks and Tulsa based Williams Companies who provided employee matching gifts to encourage charitable support.

We worked diligently to validate these various efforts to be sure they could guarantee the funds would be coming to us for the purpose outlined by the Stillwater Strong Committee and we created third-party forms to ensure we had contact information and other required details to guarantee the unknown offers were legitimate.

More than one of the regular football tailgating groups collected donations from fans and asked me to join them for a presentation. This is just one of those groups who stepped up to honor and support tragedy victims.

BEDLAM BUCKETS

A plea went out to the eighty living Pistol Pete Alumni members, Stillwater Medical personnel, the entire OSU spirit squad, student groups from Stillwater High School, and other volunteers. We needed help. It would be a vast effort to organize the passing of the buckets at the Bedlam football game, secure the funds, and count the money.

Keegan Davis with the OSU Posse Office in the athletic department thoughtfully provided tickets to those volunteers who were not season ticket holders to help encourage their assistance. Our volunteer groups gathered an hour before kickoff to get the bucket routine instructions.

A bitter cold Bedlam evening could have dampened the atmosphere, but the loyal and true Cowboy fans stepped up, warming our hearts in vivid Poke spirit. Even Sooner fans sprinkled throughout Boone Pickens Stadium contributed to the cause.

Two people were assigned to every section: lower, middle, upper, and to the club level of the stadium. When Larry announced the event over the Pickens Stadium public address system, the buckets were passed row by row, permitting people to insert coins, cash, and checks. The athletic department even had a staff member deliver Stillwater Strong envelopes in the suite level.

The bucket lids were extremely tight so no one could pop one off to help themselves to the collection. To ensure we managed the funds properly, the proven system was used with two people collecting and then two people walking all of the funds to the designated door at the OSU Athletic Center. The locked OSU Ticket Office vault secured the money ensuring protection until Monday morning when it could be counted and processed.

The Monday following Bedlam at 9 a.m., I met Larry and Keegan, the guys who orchestrated this effort. The funds had been condensed from scores of plastic buckets into three large cardboard boxes. We loaded them into the covered bed of my truck and locked the tailgate. We weren't taking any chances.

I advised the bank we would be arriving with the boxes of money and they directed us where to go. Like Brinks armored guards, the three of us marched the boxes stuffed full of cash, checks, and coins into BankSNB and transferred the boxes through a secured deposit process.

Multiple bank staff spent all of Monday and even part of Tuesday morning, flattening, counting and recounting the bills. They had machines to expedite the process while we contemplated the amount collected. $10,000? $20,000? To our elation, the Bedlam bucket passing totaled over $43,000!

Thanks to the generosity of our bedlam attendees, we had quickly exceeded an anonymous challenge match we announced two days earlier on Thanksgiving Day. Now we would be receiving another $40,000 from an anonymous donor.

Courtesy of Stillwater Strong

After participating in passing the bucket with approximately 100 other volunteers, Catherine Petty and her boyfriend Matt Arrington posed with two unidentified fans in the east end-zone at the OSU vs. OU Bedlam football game on Nov. 28, 2015. On this night, generous Cowboy and Sooner fans raised over $43,000 for homecoming crash victims.

THE HARRISON FAMILY

I will forever be grateful to David Harrison for his patience throughout our search for his daughter, Kelly, and his ability to deal positively with the chaos of this event. He and Suzie had both of their adult daughters move back into their home so they could help them literally get back on their feet.

They have raised two incredibly positive young women. From the first visit with them in their hospital rooms they exuded a remarkable spirit and enthusiasm about making a full recovery. Discussing their plans for physical therapy and the journey toward walking again was simply inspirational. Zero conversation took place regarding, "why this occurred," or "how the slightest movements in another direction could have killed both siblings." They kept focused on the future and progressing forward beyond this temporary side-step.

Less than thirty days after the crash, David and Suzie along with their two daughters Kelly and Kimberly attended our Stillwater Medical Foundation gala dinner and auction. One of their first times to venture out of their home together after they both landed in wheel chairs, they joined us in raising funds for our Total Fitness Aquatics pool and the Stillwater Strong Fund effort. Though both young ladies were unable to walk during this stage of their recovery, they still accepted the invitation to attend our special evening, and I was delighted they wanted to dress up and attend.

THE FOUNDATION

Less than one month after the crash, at the Stillwater Medical Foundation's regularly scheduled board meeting, a subcommittee was appointed to review and recommend a model for distribution of the Stillwater Strong Fund. Though we had no hint of how large it could grow, we knew we wanted multiple perspectives and broad-thinking minds to consider the distribution process, timing, and publicity.

This group met several times, reviewing the steps and processes other organizations used to benefit those injured in the Murrah Federal Building bombing as well as the tragedies in both New York City and Boston.

We began to receive inquiries from victims about the timing of distribution as early as November. In early December, we promoted the fact that we were ending the effort on December 31, 2015, so that we could distribute these funds to victims who had been off work and needing to pay bills.

The subcommittee concluded we would work to end the effort and fully distribute all funds within the next several months. With legal counsel's guidance, letters were still required from victims agreeing to accept the funds.

Since we had never before collected funds benefitting victims of a mass tragedy, the Stillwater Medical Foundation engaged with a local attorney to help ensure we were managing the Stillwater Strong effort properly. Thanks to another attorney already serving on our board we understood directing funds to the families with children injured would require a "Transfer to Minors" release document that the parents would be required to sign saying they would accept these funds on behalf of their minor children.

However, there were several complicated issues to answer. As a small foundation established for the primary purpose of providing funds for employee scholarships, equipment, and building projects for the hospital, this certainly wasn't our field of forte.

Unsure of exactly how many people had been injured, our team methodically examined public records, from police reports to court records. We worked diligently, thoroughly vetting individuals and including those qualified, excluding those who weren't. We communicated multiple times with the families double-checking names and addresses of those documented individuals.

Our group decided we did not want to apply a value to the severity of injuries or loss of life. We had some very thoughtful discussions about what made the most sense and why. The conclusion to create three distinct classes defining how the funds would be distributed took time and careful consideration.

First, we prioritized and settled on the amount of a reasonable funeral service and burial. One of our committee members had just experienced the loss of a young life in his own family, so his personal insight was exceptionally helpful. Once we knew the range of a reasonable funeral, we added additional funds to the bottom line. We then determined there would be two classes relating to the injured.

Though a few victims were admitted and spent the night, or even multiple nights at Stillwater Medical Center, we knew those who had been treated and released from either Stillwater Medical or Perry Memorial Hospital, did not experience life-threatening injury. The victims whom had been flown to Tulsa or Oklahoma City, had either serious trauma or life-threatening conditions that needed to be cared for at a trauma center.

Fifty-one days after the crash, we had deposited $383,531.53 into the Stillwater Strong account where we kept the funds separate from the other charitable gifts for other hospital priorities. By not co-mingling funds we were able to precisely track money deposited, ensuring 100% of those dollars would go directly to the parade victims or their surviving family members.

THE BATES FAMILY

Her memory recall began around the week she was discharged in Oklahoma City. Paul Bates was allowed to transport his wife to Tulsa to begin her rehabilitation. Sheri was released to Kaiser Rehabilitation where she underwent five days of inpatient rehab until she was finally released to go home the day before Thanksgiving.

Upon their arrival at Kaiser Rehabilitation, Paul and a nurse helped Sheri transfer from the truck into a wheelchair. While Paul parked the truck, the nurse wheeled Sheri into her room on the first floor.

Sheri was overcome with emotion and began to cry.

"Oh, please don't cry, don't cry it's okay. We'll take great care of you," the nurse said,

"I'm so sorry, I don't know why I'm upset. I'm glad to be closer to home," Sheri said.

"Oh honey, it's okay…really. This happens with a brain injury," the nurse said.

Had someone already told her she had a brain injury?

Sheri knew she was missing lots of her blonde hair, as a result of brain surgery and that she had just experienced a month of bad hair days, but a brain injury? It was like she was hearing, or remembering it for the first time. She had believed her broken femur was the biggest obstacle she faced.

Over the next week, Sheri worked diligently through her occupational and physical therapy. Even wound care was needed to guarantee she was not going to experience infections from the various traumas and recovering wounds. Though she could speak, Sheri went to speech therapy, which was more of a cognitive assessment confirming she could adequately identify pictures and easily grasp words. She had tests to make lists and worked hard to overcome her new vocally monotone inflection.

Now her focus was going home. Sheri had no idea the October morning she left her house, that it would take her two months to get back home.

Before she could be released to go home, Sheri had to learn how to care for personal needs without help from others (i.e., showering, dressing, etc.). She also learned how to walk using a walker, without putting weight on her injured left leg. She eventually used crutches and then a cane for several months. Five months after the tragedy, Sheri returned to her bank job, but only part time per doctor's restrictions.

THE WYATT AND SCHMITZ FAMILIES

Though on different floors, Leo Schmitz was also initially released to Kaiser Rehabilitation the same day as Sheri. Leo's process of recovery would be longer, as he would not only have to learn how to live with a brain injury, but he would also need to learn to walk with his prosthetic leg.

Following a brief stay at Kaiser, Leo moved to another Tulsa hospital for more recovery time. Sixty-seven days after the crash and now at Saint Francis Hospital, Sharon requested to meet with me. We visited several times about the Stillwater Strong efforts by phone, email, and text, but she invited my visit with her and Leo in his hospital room. They wanted to express their genuine thanks to everyone in Stillwater. I met Sharon and Leo Schmitz for the first time on December 30th.

They had been through the trying experiences of prayerfully awaiting surgery outcomes and then coming to grips with their new reality. Leo received twenty-seven blood donations and endured scores of surgeries, including amputation above his left knee.

Sharon met me in the Saint Francis lobby and gave me a few instructions as we walked into Leo's room. Awake on his hospital bed, Leo greeted me as if we were old friends. He reached for the remote control and turned down the bowl game on television.

"Hiiii," Leo's voice rang out hanging on to a long "I" with a broad smile. His voice still sounded raspy from the extended insertion of a breathing tube encased by his vocal chords and throat, which kept him breathing for most of his stay in Oklahoma City.

He was lying on top of the covers of his bed in a tie-dye t-shirt and wearing sweat pants with the left pant leg cutoff to reduce the possibility of entanglement. With one hand in a brace, he leaned forward shaking my hand with his good hand.

"Leo, you look just terrific," I said.

"You should have seen me before, I have lost a lot of weight," he said tilting toward me putting one hand next to his mouth as if to shield his words from Sharon. "But this isn't a weight loss plan I really endorse." Sharon, Leo, and I laughed at his good humor in the face of his daunting recovery climb.

Continuing his shtick Leo said, "I mean, talk about luck. What are the chances I'm going to get run over by a parked motorcycle?"

Amazed by his frankness-infused humor, I adored his wit.

We chatted about our successful OSU Cowboys football season and he lamented missing the homecoming and Bedlam games. Sharing what our overwhelming Cowboy Nation and Bedlam game fans had done during the bucket passing brought tears of gratitude. Sharon shook her head in amazement and indebtedness.

"Thank you. Thank you so much for what you've done to help so many," said Leo.

Inhaling like a human vacuum my lungs filled to capacity, I was unexpectedly overtaken by his emotional, heart-felt thanks. I swallowed hard feeling my chest tighten and fought back my own tears. Simultaneously, the three of us reached for the box of Kleenex at the foot of Leo's bed.

He talked about looking ahead and returning to work at American Airlines, where he has worked as a mechanic for 25 years. Given his condition and his injuries, I privately questioned the possibility of his return to that role.

I pulled from my pocket several orange silicone wristbands and Stillwater Strong lapel pins, which had the same slogan with orange ribbons on them. "These were donated by people who have been asking about you and praying for your healing. Everyone wants to wish you and your family all the best for your recovery," I said.

He began shifting around in his bed seemingly trying to scoot up, and Sharon and I instinctively helped him slide up in a better position. Sharon asked if we could take a photo. They wanted to remember everyone who visited them in the hospital.

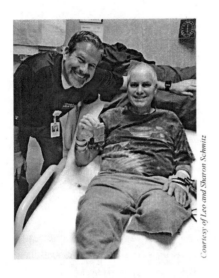

Courtesy of Leo and Sharon Schmitz

After multiple phone conversations, texts and emails, on December 30, 2015, I met Leo and Sharon for the first time during his recovery at Saint Francis Hospital in Tulsa. A smiling Leo shows off the silicone bracelets and Stillwater Strong lapel pins I delivered.

Embracing the reality of one leg, Leo talked about how he felt lucky to be alive and be with his family. He knew there were others who didn't make it, and their loved ones had no one to hold. Leo and Sharon talked about the prosthetic options. They shared the monumental cost of a prosthetic leg and how he would go through different prosthetics before receiving his own.

I described the frequent calls, donations, outpouring of love, and offers for assistance that we had received over the last two months and just how glad I was to get to meet "Leo the Super Hero" in person. That's the term the Wyatt family coined Leo after they learned he saved Hadley's life.

Christmas morning, Sara and Adam Wyatt loaded the girls in their SUV in Chattanooga, Oklahoma, leaving the southwest corner of Oklahoma. They made the 215-mile trek up Interstate 44 to Tulsa for one of their most memorable Christmas experiences a youthful family could have.

A journey befitting the mystique of The Polar Express, Hadley and Mia were thrilled to see Leo awake for the first time. Sara and Adam believed it would be a fulfilling gift to their girls, but now hearing the Schmitz' enthusiasm about the opportunity to spend time with the young Wyatt family it clearly illuminated their own fulfillment. Each gave the other hope when hope looked bleak.

Except for her own frequent doctor appointments with specialists in Oklahoma City, Hadley had made a strong recovery and returned to school most of the last two months. While Leo laid in a coma the majority of the time he was in the OKC hospital, he was visited by Hadley and her family multiple times.

The Wyatts bonded with Sharon. They felt a kinship with Leo after learning crash video showed his body shielding Hadley from the catapulting motorcycle.

The Wyatt family learned of Leo's progress and transfer to the Tulsa hospital for physical therapy and in preparation for his computerized, prosthetic leg. The Wyatts decided to make their family's Christmas present to each other a special road trip to Tulsa to visit the Schmitz'.

The Wyatt's visit to Leo's Tulsa hospital room on December 25th, provided healing for the young Wyatt family as much as for Sharon and Leo. Now they were forever friends.

Leo expressed to me how much he enjoyed their visit only five days earlier and looked forward to going home, or at least being released to initiate physical therapy and walk again. Being on his back and unresponsive for so long made him enthusiastic to begin his journey onward to find a new normal.

A KEY STORY

Vice-President of Student Affairs at Oklahoma State University, Dr. Lee Bird not only has years of experience as an EMT, but also with helping students deal with academic challenges or personal tragedy. She spends much time leading and inspiring students, a friend to those needing a shoulder. She is a problem solver, a 'get it done yesterday,' kind of personality, who focuses on successful outcomes of collegians.

In our Foundation board meetings, Dr. Bird is regularly known to be the first expressing emphatically, "so moved," when a motion for minutes approval is sought. She staunchly fights for students' rights and expresses a deep compassion when fitting.

During the chaos on the day of the homecoming crash, Lee and I encountered each other in a back hallway at Stillwater Medical. "Scott, do you know where I can find some pliers?" Dr. Bird asked. "I need to fix something."

The request was a little odd and I was extremely distracted at the time; however, I would do anything for Dr. B. "Well, I'm sure there are some surgical tools around here, but I guess it depends what you're going to do with them. Do you actually need pliers?" I asked.

I couldn't imagine what in the world she would be fixing in our hospital in the middle of this catastrophic recovery event. She possibly told me specifically what she needed them for, but my mind raced with other images: the last hallway, a friend waiting with a bloodied patient. I didn't fully process her request.

Over two months later, while standing in Leo's Saint Francis hospital room in Tulsa, his wife, Sharon, began telling a story.

"Oh, Scott, one of the funniest things happened and maybe you can tell us who helped us," she said.

"Our car key was in Leo's pocket and when the impact of the car impaled the motorcycle into him, the car key in his pocket was bent in a perfect 90° angle. Someone in your hospital was able to bend it back," she continued. Showing me her index finger she straightened it from 90° to the perfect universal signal for 'we're number one!'

"Our daughter-in-law, Angela, dynamically gesturing from across the intersection, literally played charades with our son, Mark, reminding him to get the car key out of Leo's pocket as he was being loaded into the helicopter. They took the damaged key with them to Stillwater Medical," Sharon paused. "An amazing woman at the hospital was able to bend it back. Do you know who our "Key Lady" is?"

Immediately, problem-solver and fix-it, Lee "Pliers" Bird came to mind.

"Was it possibly Dr. Lee Bird," I asked.

"Yes, I think it was Lee Bird," Sharon exclaimed. She had heard so many names and so many people offered help over the days, weeks, and months following the accident.

"I have no idea how she was able to do it, but she saved the day and the key worked in the car that day and still does. This is the key." Sharon proudly held the key up, showing it as though she had just performed a circus act. I heard a ta-daa inside my head as she showed me the key.

THE HARRISON FAMILY

Less than two months after the crash, though still in physical therapy both girls were thriving. Dr. Wuller released Kimberly to return to her banking job as a customer service trainer at RCB Bank, and Kelly was preparing to return to her doctoral studies at the University of Kansas.

Kimberly's leg had to stay straight at zero degrees in a wheel chair at work to avoid bending her reconstructed knee. She evolved to crutches, but non-weight bearing, so she was still getting around on the walker at home. Kimberly excelled in physical therapy and though not physically ready, she wanted to lead a "normal life" once again. However, she still had to depend upon her mom to wash her hair in the kitchen sink since she couldn't navigate the shower. Kimberly's beloved cat named "Lola" knew Suzie washing her daughter's hair in the sink wasn't normal.

The cat jumped up on the counter crying and swiping at Suzie's hand while she mothered her daughter back to health. But Lola knew this wasn't acceptable to Kimberly. Lola wanted to put a stop to it and wanted her normal cat-loving owner back.

Kelly, technically still a teaching assistant at the University of Kansas, while going through the rigors of physical therapy in Stillwater, had already returned to grading papers and working on her PhD from afar living in her parents' home. Kelly's boss brought her laptop to Oklahoma so she could continue progress toward her ultimate goal of walking across that stage and defending her dissertation.

Finally, able to return to Lawrence, Kansas, and still unable to adequately navigate stairs, Kelly Harrison moved out of her 3rd floor apartment to a 1st floor unit. Thankfully, the Red Cross chipped in helping her family relocate her to a new downstairs home.

THE MURPHY FAMILY

The fact that Kelly D. Murphy was in Tulsa's St. John's Intensive Care Unit for only three full days seems surreal to her. Surgeons told Kelly D. that no two traumatic injuries are identical. "We don't know what your healing will look like," her surgeon said. With a serious concussion and two severely broken legs mended with a workbench of high-dollar hardware accessories, Kelly D. felt a personal note of thanks to Ace Hardware might be warranted.

Around 75 days after the crash, she was still not driving a car. With growing cabin fever, Kelly D. wanted to be with her boot camp girlfriends for support and inspiration and just plain friendship. Her friend, Alane Zannotti, picked her up at her house at 5:30 a.m., three days a week, taking her to boot camp to watch her girlfriends workout. She eventually graduated from wheelchair, to walker, unable to sit long with her knees bent.

With rods running the length of her tibias and screws in her both of her ankles and her knees, she had begun to feel whole again, when she decided it was time to push herself.

One morning, while still just an inspirational observer at boot camp, Kelly D. made up her mind she was going to try to jump. Her girlfriends all gathered around her in support. Kelly D. held her breath, and she jumped. She did it, but it hurt! At a future checkup with her trauma surgeon, she said in very matter of fact tone to her doctor, "Oh, I jumped in boot camp the other day."

"You what?!" Her surgeon half-questioned, half-exclaimed. Surprised by his own response, the doctor continued with more control, "Well, I really wouldn't recommend it."

"I have patients hesitant to even try walking again, so I'll use your story to illustrate that there are those trying to jump back into life and those who want life to jump back into them," said the doctor.

THE HUGHES FAMILY

The Harrison sisters performed months of intense physical therapy together. A physical therapist from Stillwater Medical's Total Health division named Lisa Hughes, worked daily beside the sisters. Lisa provided elements of psychological inspiration, as well as physical techniques, helping the Harrison sisters and another OSU crash victim to recovery. A painfully long, arduous process, Lisa channeled a silently selfish interest in getting these ladies to thrive.

Lisa's daughter, Bella Kate, had been feet from the mad chaos the morning lives were shattered. The child seated in the grass next to Synnove Talley was her daughter. Hers was the other child Justin Talley helped safely seat in the grass as that speeding vehicle altered humanity. Scooping up both Bella Kate and Synnove, Justin had jogged through the dazed crowd carrying them both to safety.

Like most in the profession of physical recovery, this physical therapist has always taken her job seriously and with the deepest compassion. Lisa derives enormous satisfaction helping patients recover physically and providing them the ability to return to work, or regain as normal an existence as humanly possible.

She was doing this not only for the patients and her career, but for her little, 7-year-old love. Bella Kate needed to know the victims who survived such a physical atrocity were going to recover. Lisa had a burning desire to help her daughter see that though four deeply loved people died, those injured could experience a physical renewal.

Lisa's passion became a mission of hope for more than just the Harrison sisters. Her own flesh and blood was watching from a distance to see if these victims really could one day heal and prosper.

Kelly officially completed her physical therapy twelve months and one day after the crash. In hindsight, running a 5K race to celebrate the twelve-month anniversary of her recovery could have been slightly aggressive, but she was inspired and determined to bounce back with passion.

Unfortunately, Kelly developed a tibia plateau fracture in one of her legs from pushing herself a bit too hard. Fifteen months after the crash, Kelly had gone two steps forward and one step back. Her wheelchair confinement lasted four more weeks so her tibia could heal again. Kelly's unwavering resilience for complete recovery and her positive passion to heal won and just ahead, there were even more wins.

THE STONE FAMILY

Flagler, Colorado, resident Lenny Stone, a surviving brother of homecoming victim Marvin Stone said, "Tragedy has molded an unbelievable culture of compassion in Stillwater."

Marvin, a renowned professor emeritus in the department of Biosystems and Agricultural Engineering, continued teaching his students well after his 20 years of service to Oklahoma State University and retirement. Bonnie, his wife, was a coordinator for Student Information Systems in the Office of Institutional Research and Information Management, a position she held for nearly 20 years.

Lenny, his siblings, and their 90-year-old mother, have been humbled beyond words by the outpouring of love and benevolence their family experienced in the days that followed the deaths of Marvin and Bonnie Stone.

The Stone family ultimately made a decision positively impacting nineteen other families of those seriously wounded in the homecoming crash that would authentically and forever etch the notion of paying it forward into this sad event. The Stone family was one of a handful of families who kindly declined the distribution of Stillwater Strong funds thereby helping to ease the pain for others.

Those charitable gifts would have helped bury their loved ones, but the Stones thought of survivors with mounting medical bills, facing uncertain medical futures who might be aided even more if they decided to pay it forward. The generosity of the Stone Family and others vaulted immeasurable compassion exceeding what anyone may have expected. In fact, other than a few victims, most never knew about these unselfish acts of true generosity.

THE SCHMITZ FAMILY

The new year came and time passed. I had forgotten about the revelation in the hospital room, when Sharon Schmitz remembered Dr. Lee Bird was the one who straightened out their car key. Months later, the OU Health Center invited several surviving victims from the homecoming tragedy and various Stillwater entities to be honored at a reception including, Stillwater Medical, Stillwater Police, Stillwater Fire, LifeNet EMS, and Stillwater Emergency Management. Annually, they hold this event for a collection of special survivors and victims so those involved in the line of lifesaving work can see the success stories from their labor.

Stillwater Medical Center staff and crash victims (fourth from right) Annette Turner, Hadley Wyatt, and Leo Schmitz celebrate the Golden Hour Award from the OU Medical Center.

There were victims who had been in serious accidents like the man run over by his own tractor. These harrowing life experiences and the life-saving stories that accompanied them were equally powerful. Victims' stories of survival coupled with the perspectives of the trauma surgeons who saved their lives provide unparalleled insight into why people in healthcare and first responders do what they do.

I went along to support our local legends and see new friends, Hadley and Leo and their families, who were continuing to heal both physically and emotionally. At the conclusion of the Friday evening event in Oklahoma City, the Schmitz' told me they would be coming to Stillwater the next day and would really like to connect again if our schedules permitted. We made plans and met up.

They asked me to join them while Leo visited a teenage boy, who had recently lost his leg in a motorcycle accident. I didn't want to impose, but Sharon insisted it would be good for me to meet this local family.

Leo now makes these visits frequently because he knows how important it is to show that recovering and being positive again is possible. He is personally a terrific success story especially in light of his brain injury and being in a medically induced coma for much of two months.

Leo imparts the right amount of humor and sincerity in these personal visits, so he's a bit like a one-legged Pistol Pete. The fact that Leo literally used to dress like a clown to entertain people of all ages isn't a surprise to anyone who has met him.

Still clowning around for smiles, today Leo sheds hope and light into the eyes and hearts of victims experiencing a personal tragedy. He does this hoping to inspire those who are just beginning to grasp the gravity and reality that they will need to learn things all over again.

During our conversation with this Stillwater family, and the boy who as it turned out was also in my son's high school senior class, Sharon brought up the story of their car key repair again.

"I sure would like to thank Dr. Bird for saving the day by bending our key back into place so Mark could get our car," Leo said.

"Dr. Bird lives just around the corner from me. I've got her number. Do you want me to call her and see if she is able to meet us this afternoon?" I asked.

"Well sure, if you don't mind. Do you think she'll see us on her Saturday? It really would be a treat for us to tell her thank you in person," Sharon said.

I stepped away and called Dr. Bird's cell phone to tell her who I was with and what we were doing.

"Oh Scott, I'm covered in grass and grease because I've been mowing and working in the yard today. If they can handle seeing me in my other work clothes sure, come on over," Dr. Bird said.

Minutes later we pulled up to the curb near Dr. Bird's home, where she and a friend were standing in the driveway beside her trusty riding lawn mower. It meant so much to the Schmitz' to hug Dr. Bird's neck and tell her thank you.

The visit touched everyone. I'm not sure whom the visit impacted most, but reflecting on the paths forever intertwining these lives was profound.

Leading college students and supervising those who manage the nearly 400 Oklahoma State clubs and organizations keeps Dr. Bird on her toes. I've never seen tears in her eyes. However, that afternoon it wasn't the orange dust from her grass clippings and mower. The fact that the Schmitz' wanted to see and personally thank her, rewarded her beyond expectation. Once again, Lee had a hand in helping someone special find the strength in their first healing steps.

Standing near Dr. Lee Bird's home, from left, Sharon Schmitz, Lee, and Leo reconnect approximately seven months after the crash.

Often when Leo Schmitz awoke, he didn't remember conversations and visits from people. He remembered nothing after standing at the homecoming parade until waking up in his hospital bed with only one leg. With Leo's amazing progress in the coming months, he proudly resumed work at American Airlines' maintenance facility in Tulsa, Oklahoma, less than eight months after the crash.

Receiving a true hero's welcome his first day back, hundreds of the same fellow employees who rallied behind him, greeted him as he humbly strode into a giant hangar full of cheering and applauding friends. In the preceding months, he learned that thousands of the American Airlines family had been prayerfully lifting up Sharon and Leo, as well as Sheri and Paul Bates, for strength in their recovery.

Today's technology gives amputees a controllable prosthetic. A computerized leg, a C-Leg, permits an app on Leo's smart phone to communicate with it. He is able to track battery power of his leg and adjust its strength settings with a few finger strokes of his iPhone. If walking upstairs or performing other strenuous activities he can adjust the leg's power with his fingertip.

Leo steps with a revitalized confidence using his C-Leg as he scales stairs, crosses aircraft bulkheads, and continues working to keep their fleet of aircraft serving American Airlines' customers. "Leo the Super Hero" has made it his mission to visit new amputee victims to impart his message of acceptance, progress, and hope.

Nine months after the crash, Sheri Bates joined a group of "teenyboppers" her daughter's age, to be evaluated by a driving instructor to prove she was capable of being responsive and sharp enough to follow the rules of the road. She wasn't released to drive until nearly ten months after she sustained her Traumatic Brain Injury.

Returning to work brought new challenges, the first of which was transportation to and from the bank. Sheri's parents had stayed with her during her days of recovery at home, so their role naturally transitioned into that of driving her to work mid-morning each day that she was scheduled. At first, her parents would arrive together to take Sheri. As the days and weeks passed, Sheri's mom began to stay home. She wanted to give Sheri and her dad time together. He had worked so hard when Sheri and her siblings were growing up that he missed out on opportunities like this.

Her Dad relished the opportunity to drive over from Owasso to take his sweet Sheri to her job in Oologah. After all, she was alive and when her parents first got the call of the tragedy they wondered if life would ever be the same for their family.

The daily routine became a time of sharing for both Sheri and her dad, talking about life, love, and family. This father/daughter time was unexpectedly sweeter and more fulfilling than either of them could have imagined. Neither of them could have envisioned a reason for them to spend this unexpected quality time together in this stage of life. It was simply an unexpected bonus and an indescribable blessing.

At the end of Paul's shift at American Airlines he would swing by the bank to pick her up on his way home and they would share details about their workday. In the momentarily childless solitude of their five mile windshield encased drive time, which they honestly hadn't experienced since early in their 26 year marriage, they shared a new appreciation for each other and for life. Being reinstated to full time employment 22 months after the crash seemed like an eternity, but her bank family held her position and patiently welcomed her with open arms.

ONE YEAR AFTER THE CRASH

Kelly D. Murphy's intense pain never really went away. So about ten months after the crash, she had another CT scan, and it was determined her injury had become a "non-union," which means the bone stays broken. Though she grew new bone it wasn't going to heal properly. The surgeon knew immediately it would require another surgery at St. John's, and the same surgeon who cared for her the first time would dive in for a second surgery on both of Kelly D's legs.

Homecoming crash survivors get a visit from OSU Mascot, Pistol Pete. (Left of Pete) Kelly D. Murphy and (Right) Diana Rodriguez, attend a Cowboy Basketball game shortly after Homecoming 2016. A surprise visit from Pistol Pete spread smiles all around. (Far left) Pete Alumni, D. Scott Petty 1985-87 and (far right) Taylor Collins, Pete 2015-17 share the evening.

Courtesy of Stillwater Strong

Following her surgery twelve months after the crash, she stayed out of boot camp not just because her legs were very swollen, but because she knew three months of healing time wasn't enough to just "jump back in." She attended OSU's Homecoming 2016 in a wheelchair, recovering from that surgery, patiently awaiting her opportunity to walk again.

Kelly Harrison ran that 5K celebrating her healing journey. Though suffering through a lingering knee issue and likely facing another surgery in the near future, this survivor embraces every step in her new life.

Nineteen months after the crash, she walked across the stage for her hooding at the University of Kansas receiving her PhD in biosciences with a focus in infectious diseases. With three "dream job" offers on the table, Kelly was preparing to defend her dissertation 21 months after the crash.

Nearly two years after she and her sister, Kimberly, were rendered temporarily confined to wheelchairs and unable to walk, she joined Oklahoma State University and the School of Veterinary Medicine. She was drawn to that opportunity by forces of goodwill, love, and an incomparable community of family. She was all orange; she was a POKE!

REUNION OF UNEXPECTED FRIENDS

Nearly one year to the day of the crash, just one week before the Oklahoma State University Homecoming of 2016, Director of Stillwater Emergency Management Rob Hill, second year Pistol Pete Taylor Collins, Leo and Sharon Schmitz, Hadley Wyatt along with her sister, Mia, and parents, Adam and Sara, and others sat down for a conversation with an Oklahoma City television anchor to hold a reunion of sorts.

The gathering served as a chance for a couple of seriously injured victims, first responders and those involved both during and after the crash, to come together for a time of reflection. On this day, a powerfully emotional reconnection gave friends an opportunity to express appreciation for each other, providing a path of continued healing. They hugged, cried, and expressed an unabridged gratitude for the countless people who unselfishly stepped forward to help.

The week of OSU's 2016 Homecoming, inside the Oklahoma City studios of ABC Affiliate TV Station KOCO, the Schmitz and Wyatt Families gathered to reflect on their last 12 months. First responders and volunteers who worked the scene, and others who worked at Stillwater Medical were also present that day sharing their perspectives.

The 2016 OSU Sea of Orange Homecoming Parade was led by three saddled horses and one pony. None of the horses had riders. Each led by a law enforcement officer walking as an honor guard leading each riderless horse. Those four horses began the parade representing and honoring the shortened lives of Nikita Nakal, Bonnie and Marvin Stone and the pony was in honor of little Nash Lucas. Their somber presence was meant for us to remember them. Forever gone from this life. It will be up to us to remember the impact they had on us and how they touched Oklahoma State University and the community of Stillwater.

Four Payne County Sheriff's Department Officers lead three horses and a small pony adorned with a bouquet of orange roses down the center of Main Street twelve months after the crash. Each of the horses had a pair of orange and black boots reverse mounted in the saddle stirrups honoring the four killed one year earlier.

The OSU Homecoming Student Committee chose Parade Marshalls who represented first responders, medical personnel, law enforcement, and those directly involved in providing recovery efforts for the victims. Scores of parade goers applauded while wiping back sentimental tears for their work in the heat of the battle. Thousands lining the streets gave thumbs up acknowledging a job well done.

The dream for the 2016 OSU Homecoming celebration was for it to come off without a hitch. For there to be no unexpected event. For there to be no sudden sadness and no tragic ending. There would be no rain on this parade. On this day, the sun and nearly twelve months of time helped to begin healing the wounds and the void created by the cruel loss of life. Our 2016 OSU Homecoming was both a great success and the renewal of hope.

Courtesy of Adam and Sara Wyatt

Both boasting Pistol Pete tattooed cheeks. (L to R, front) Mia and Hadley Wyatt celebrate the 2016 Homecoming with OSU Spirit Squad members (L to R), Hallie Light and Makynna Edwards, whom they met by chance twelve months earlier. This was a homecoming highlight for each of these four young ladies.

2016 OSU HOMECOMING QUEEN CANDIDATE

Ultimately, the Oklahoma State University Student Government Association's motivated effort led by those two driven students, contributed more than any single donor to the Stillwater Strong cause. The t-shirt visionary, Jacquelyn Lane, later admitted that she thought they might be able to sell 1,000 shirts. However, the simple, student-inspired design sold an astonishing 10,000 units.

That single t-shirt, on which they collaborated and partnered with Eskimo Joe's Promotional Products Group and Joe's Clothes raised over $82,000, an amazing success and a true blessing for the victims. This effort provided the largest individual donation to the Stillwater Strong Fund.

Almost one year to the day after the 2015 homecoming crash, I sat alone in my Boone Pickens Stadium seat during the 2016 homecoming halftime festivities. My family retreated for a snack while the Cowboy Marching Band performed their halftime show. Like clockwork, homecoming winners from various OSU living groups were swiftly shuttled on and off the field recognized with a quick photo op during this tight window between the second and third quarters of the football game.

As sororities and fraternities are honored for their winning house decorations, parade float creations, and other collegiate competitions, anticipation built for the announcement of the next homecoming queen. Since I learned of Jacquelyn's selection as a homecoming queen candidate a few weeks earlier, I wanted to take in this moment. Like many, I searched for another light of hope helping OSU emerge from the darkness that twisted 2015's homecoming into a bitter memory.

Competition for the recognition of OSU's Homecoming Queen is significant given the leadership qualities of the candidates involved. From my perspective, Jacquelyn being honored as a member of the homecoming court was recognition well-deserved.

The physical and emotional agony those crash victims and their families were working through still creates immeasurable challenges. Like their recoveries, if Jacquelyn were honored as homecoming queen, it likely would not make any headlines. Honestly, not many knew she and her friends helped quarterback such a homecoming comeback.

This young lady helped inspire a movement within the OSU student body, alumni, and throughout the Stillwater community. Her maturity and compassion, her parent's inspiration, and kindheartedness for others instilled in her a belief that paying-it-forward, doing the right thing, and being loyal and true would make a difference.

Jacquelyn stood on the football field along with four other ladies and their five male counterparts. Each of those student leaders represented excellence in academics and service. A brief bio provided a thumbnail sketch of who these students were.

Before the introduction of OSU's Homecoming Queen and King, Jacquelyn's mind flashed back. In her homecoming queen application bio, her childhood dream was to be a Disney Princess. Possessing an ideal blend of poised charm and regal elegance inspired thoughts of one day actually dawning a crown.

Standing at midfield awaiting the homecoming king and queen's names to be ballyhooed seemed highly flattering. Being selected and attainting the recognition to stand on the field seemed like honor enough if another student's name was called. But, when she heard, "Our 2016 OSU Homecoming Queen is— a Chemical Engineering Senior from Beulah, Colorado, Jacquelyn Lane." She was stunned.

Wondering if she heard the PA announcer correctly, her head swiveled now eye to eye with her escort, Ridge Howell. Jacquelyn bit her lip rather than blurting out, "Come again?!" Applause erupted as that announcement filtered her entire being.

A majority contingent of the fans in Boone Pickens Stadium cheered in elation. From my seat in the stands, I got a chill and tears filled my eyes. Doing the right thing and thriving on the opportunity to pay it forward, she excelled in finding light in the darkness. It wasn't all about Jacquelyn, it truly was about her service. She symbolically modeled what the student body and OSU alumni everywhere had hoped for since the last homecoming celebration. Just as in her favorite quote from Eleanor Roosevelt, "It is better to light a candle than curse the darkness."

In the closing days of her senior year, Jacquelyn Lane received the high distinction as one of OSU's sixteen Outstanding Seniors in the class of 2017. Her graduating class will go down in OSU history with many dedicated leaders, creative innovators, and inspired Pokes of pivotal promise! Jacquelyn was in the right place at the right time and what a difference she made for being a human that had the determination and strength to "do the right thing."

Courtesy of Gary Lawson

Twelve months after the crash, 2016 OSU Homecoming Queen, Jacquelyn Lane, and Homecoming King, Ridge Howell, were honored at mid-field inside Boone Pickens Stadium.

THE END

*"The best way to find yourself,
is to lose yourself in the service of others."*

Mahatma Gandhi

EPILOGUE

December 15, 2015
Stillwater Strong Plan was presented, discussed and approved by the Stillwater Medical Foundation Board of Directors

- Following approval of the plan for the Stillwater Strong Fund we communicated with numerous stakeholders before the end of December to determine the identities and current contact information for individuals eligible for disbursement in accordance with the defined plans. These individuals fell into three distinct categories. Those three groups were:

  • Those who perished from their injuries
  • Those severely injured or whom would likely have long term recovery
  • Those who were treated and released

- During the week of December 15, 2015, the individuals in all three of these distinct groups were initially notified in writing, by letter of their eligibility to receive a one-time disbursement as well as other important information.

  • The opportunity was given for victims to decline the one-time disbursement and pay it forward to other victims.
  • A notification was sent about potential tax ramifications and directions for those individuals receiving disbursement on behalf of a minor child.
  • Additional communication in writing was made to individuals who did not respond within the time frame allotted.

February 17, 2016
The first disbursement of funds to the victims commenced.
  - 41 victims and victims' family members accepted distributions

March 15, 2016
The Stillwater Medical Foundation staff had received all requested information from all anticipated recipients or their representatives.

March 30, 2016
The last disbursement was made to the final recipient.

Total donated to the SMF and redistributed was $485,395.04

All costs associated with the administration of the disbursements including postage, bank charges, legal, and other fees associated with this project were paid from the SMF's general fund and were not deducted from the Stillwater Strong funds.

In accordance with the plan approved by the SMF Board, any donations received by the Foundation after February 29, 2016, designated to Stillwater Strong would be directed to the Foundation's SMC Emergency Department Fund and donors were notified of this direction.

REMEMBERING

Nash Conrad Lucas
April 24, 2013
Weatherford, OK

Courtesy of Niki Strauch

Nash was a sweet, happy and energetic toddler. He loved everyone fiercely and had an infectious smile that could turn any day around. Nash was from Weatherford, Oklahoma. He was only 2-years-old and the impact of his life story had only just begun.

Learning about the tragically abbreviated life of this special little soul numbed our University and our community. No matter how daunting the pain for our community at large, it pales in comparison to the void left for his surviving Mother, Niki Strauch, his Father, Josh Lucas, and their extended family and friends. Nash was an important life to many. A blossom lost well before full bloom.

Nikita Prabhakar Nakal
January 20, 1992
Mumbai, India

Nikita's decision to fly to America to earn her MBA, created an uneasiness for her mother. Several aircraft tragedies in 2015, heightened her apprehension about Nikita flying abroad. Though Nikita didn't like the idea of traveling aboard an airplane for multiple hours either, she loved the idea of spreading her wings to fulfill her academic dream in the United States.

However, her fears were eliminated by her boyfriend, Bhardwaj Varma. Nikita and Bhardwaj met in 2012, while working at JP Morgan Chase in Mumbai, India. Though they were both accepted to multiple universities in the United States. Bhardwaj was accepted into the Master's program at OSU for Quantitative Finance, while Nikita accepted her offer to attend the University of Central Oklahoma. He would be by her side virtually the entire way helping her navigate her way to the U.S., and he would only be about forty-five minutes away, from his door to hers.

Unchartered territory for the Nakal family, they had no idea the day she left India would be the last day they would see her alive in person. Fortunately, Nikita would Skype with her family back in India every day. Each day they would talk about what they did today and what they were going to do tomorrow. They were a tightknit family.

Today, they long for the beautiful daughter they had hopes would one day bring them grandchildren. Nikita passed from this life with Bhardwaj by her side in the middle of Main Street after enjoying that historic college parade. Due to medical examiner limitations and the various customs processing requirements, it took Nikita's body four days to ultimately travel to India. Bhardwaj accompanied her body on the flight, so he would arrive home at the same time. The excruciating wait for her return to India would be a secondary bitter life transition, difficult for the Nakal family to accept after Bhardwaj had to make that shocking late night phone call.

Her brother, Nishith, lost his only sister and they were siblings whom confided in one another. With Nikita's beautiful smile and shy sincerity now gone, her mother has experienced several health problems brought on by the deepening sadness of their family's loss.

The friends Nikita made during her brief time in the United States were genuine. Those friends dearly miss her and understood her dream to return to India to live close to and perhaps one day provide even more for her family.

Her boyfriend, Bhardwaj, completed his MBA in Quantitative Finance at Oklahoma State University in May of 2017. Even today, he feels an enormous void with her loss and wishes he could have taken the brunt of the crash. He and Nikita were hopeful to marry one day. Bhardwaj knows she wouldn't have come to the U.S. for graduate school had he not encouraged her. An unrelenting guilt works through his heart and not a day goes by that he doesn't think about her.

Nikita's father, Prabhakar, closed his automotive parts business as everything he built was for their future family. Nikita now gone, her father, too, has lost his professional passion.

To this day, Bhardwaj's loyalty for the Nakal family still shines brightly. He speaks to one of Nikita's family members every few days. She is in his thoughts always and her memory gives him strength to move forward.

He contemplates how different life would be had that one day been different in some small way. Had they chosen to stand even three or four feet in one direction or another would they both be survivors? Bhardwaj knows there was great fortune in knowing Nikita and her family. Though he obtained his master's degree, the life and death experiences that accompanied it cause him to question his decision to come to the U.S. He trusts in his faith and believes that from these experiences, one day he'll have a better grasp of this life and the impact the entire Nakal family had, not just on him, but on his family and Oklahoma State University, and the University of Central Oklahoma in Edmond, and on his own passion to help others.

Marvin and Bonnie Stone
Stillwater, OK

June 22, 1950   *February 19, 1950*

The Stones arrived on the Oklahoma State University campus in 1982. Just like their arrival together, Bonnie and Marvin departed this life together, at 65 years of age. Bonnie, loved riding her bike to campus and following her OSU Cowboy Basketball team. She derived significant satisfaction helping various University departments with new student orientation and worked in a plethora of complex IT roles. Marvin, enjoyed a highly technical career as well, thriving globally in the biomechanical engineering field through his involvement with heavy equipment. Their meaningful lives tragically ended when they were both killed instantly, together.

Bonnie served as the coordinator of Student Information Systems operations and training, a role and environment in which she thrived, through the Department of OSU's Institutional Research and Information Management. Rhoda Hughes, a Senior Technician in that department, had the privilege of working right next to her nearly every day for approximately 30 years, said, "Bonnie never liked being the center of attention. She loved devoting herself to the betterment of others. Always the first offering assistance to help with a shower, or plan a party to celebrate another person, that was Bonnie's modus operandi. Whether Boy Scout Popcorn, Girl Scout Cookies, Blue and Gold Sausage, she often bought lots of anything children were selling, whether she needed it or not."

One day, in celebration of Bonnie's birthday, the staff elaborately decorated her office reflecting their adoration for her. When Marvin saw the festive, decor done before Bonnie pedaled her way to the office for the surprise he warned very sincerely, "You know Bonnie isn't going to like this, right?" Sure enough, she expressed her displeasure and not just by simply saying, 'Oh, you shouldn't have!" Bonnie's team didn't care about causing her just a little discomfort. They enjoyed putting her in the spotlight at least sometimes to express appreciation for her relentless generosity.

Though confidential at the time, Bonnie's staff learned she quietly saved money providing much needed college tuition assistance for the son of a single parent, family friend. These and other charitable examples might explain what her supervisor, Associate VP for Institutional Research, Dr. Christie Hawkins, found while cleaning out Bonnie's office following the crash. Christie discovered a famous quote tucked with some business items on Bonnie's desk. "There is no limit to what can be achieved, if it truly doesn't matter who gets the credit." Bonnie's quote was from Theodore Roosevelt's famous, "Man In The Arena" statement. As in her life and in this example, it really did not matter who got the credit.

A Regents Professor Emeritus, Marvin retired in 2006 following a dynamic 24 years with the OSU Division of Agricultural Sciences and Natural Resources, Department of Biosystems and Agricultural Engineering. Upon retirement, Marvin frequently came to Bonnie's office in the Public Information Office Building, so they could make lunch and enjoy it together. Qualified for retirement herself, Bonnie focused her energy on helping make a new software conversion as easy as possible for her team and to her it mattered not who received the credit. Illustrating that teamwork, she even forwarded her office phone to her cell phone during a significant project. She focused on quality customer service, naturally modeling it day and night.

Marvin was a highly awarded professor who, after retirement, never truly stopped teaching. His honors and accolades read like a "Who's, Who" list for which anyone involved in academia would be humbled to share. A key contribution in which Marvin participated was the development and evolution of Oklahoma's Mesonet. The Mesonet system created through a collaborative effort between Oklahoma State University and the University of Oklahoma, tracks weather readings in all 77 Oklahoma counties, through an automated environmental monitoring network of 120 stations.

Not having children of their own, Bonnie and Marvin considered their family to be Oklahoma State students, faculty, and staff. On their last morning together, they were with their family. They knew that corner always attracted a large crowd and they adored seeing the kids' expressions of excitement. The enthusiasm of children thrilled to see bands marching, floats gliding, and shiny emergency vehicles with their dedicated, waving, and smiling public servants aboard, warmed the Stone's hearts. In fact, it is believed their standing position in the northwest corner of that intersection behind others potentially saved lives as they caught the car's numbing contact.

When Bonnie completed her thirtieth year of service as an Oklahoma State University employee, a brick in her honor was installed in the OSU garden walking path directly west of the Student Union. Later Marvin got his brick and just recently, his brick was moved so they would be next to each other just as they were in life, just as they are today.

Honoring Bonnie and Marvin's steadfast dedication to the University, the OSU departments which they served and their respective staff recently installed two sturdy wrought iron benches recognizing their important life legacy. These benches can be found near Monroe Avenue, positioned just south of the east entrance of the Public Information Office. The Stone's living example will forever be remembered by those they touched and others who visit the Stillwater Strong Memorial or rest on their benches along Monroe Avenue.

Courtesy of Jeannie Dibble

Saturday, April 7, 2018. Marvin Stone's ninety year old mother, Laura Stone, his sister, Beth Pelton and her husband, Rick, and staff from the University's Department of Institutional Research and the OSU Biosystems and Agricultural Engineering Department, gathered to dedicate the benches placed in Bonnie and Marvin's memory. Local photographer Jeannie Dibble, gave commemorative photos of the benches to the families.

A LIFETIME OF HEALING

Charged with four counts of second degree murder and 39 counts of felony assault, on January 10, 2017, a trial was to begin against the driver of the car. Rather than put the victims through the pain of a trial, through her legal counsel, the driver of the car agreed to a plea bargain. According to media accounts, the father of the female driver admitted to reporters that his daughter had received psychiatric care during an in-patient stay several years earlier.

Under the plea agreement, the driver pleaded no contest and has been sentenced to life in prison. She apologized to her victims and though many have forgiven her for her actions, the vicious void remains for four families and many others whose physical and mental health has been impacted by one person's act.

AUTHOR'S NOTE

No one person has all of the answers. Life is short. Unexpected accidents and tragic intentional events happen frequently. No one is immune to their swiftness and the ripple effect of their harsh pain. One should live with purpose, working diligently to establish a life's passion.

Love intentionally... live as if today could very well be your last. You owe it to yourself... you owe it to your loved ones... you owe it to the lives lost unexpectedly.

Every. Single. Day.

Be Stillwater Strong... stay, Loyal and True!

ACKNOWLEDGMENTS

First and foremost, I thank God that through Him all things are possible.

My wife, Gerri, and our children, Catherine and Will, exist in my life, thanks to the best decisions I've ever made. Thank you for supporting me in this whimsical journey of writing an important story for our community, our University, and our friends.

My parents, David and Sharon Petty, weathered the storm of losing my late Uncle, Donald Scott Petty, nine years before I was born and when they were only high school sweethearts. Mom and Dad, you continue to be our family's rock, and I love you. Uncle Don's story gained traction in my heart throughout my life and his tragically abbreviated time on earth is a significant reason I wanted to tell this story. A tragic passing can happen to anyone when it is least expected and sadly our Cowboy and Cowgirl fans have come to understand that better than most.

I cannot thank my sisters, Liz Lee and Crystal Byers, enough. They have been a part of my story since day one and both provided tremendous input and guidance through the writing process. You both contributed valuable critiques and you both inspire me to be a better son, brother, husband, dad, and friend.

A special thanks to Kristine Waits for helping edit multiple versions of this story before other eyes saw it. Your open-bookish encouragement and inspiration motivated me to tell this story, making it a reality.

*Thank you to my nephew, Gant Lee, Stillwater May-
or – Gina Noble, and Stillwater Public School Li-
brarian – Quinn Baldwin for your literary intelli-
gence. Your willingness to edit and ask the tough,
probing questions guided me to the goal, propelling
this dream. You each uniquely challenged me, ensuring this book had some level of appeal for potential readers.*

*Special acknowledgment to the Stillwater Strong
Committee: Dr. Lee Bird, K. Cohlmia, Jeffery
Corbett, Vic Schutte, Kenny Skillman, Amy Wells,
Mackenzie Wilfong, with assistance from Brandee
Hancock. Your guidance and service to Stillwater
Medical and the Stillwater Medical Foundation was
immeasurable.*

*The Stillwater Community Foundation board of di-
rectors accepted the request and the responsibility
to receive charitable gifts to help build the Stillwater Strong Memorial. I am thankful for your collective commitment to help honor this important memorial for the victims, Stillwater's citizens, and the
Oklahoma State University Homecoming Parade.
A special thanks to Dr. Kyle Eastham and the Stillwater Chamber of Commerce, Leadership Stillwater - Class XXVI. Coordinating the passing of the
buckets during the 2017 OSU Homecoming Football game, meant a terrific shot in the arm for the
Stillwater Strong Memorial drive. Those funds were
completely unexpected and truly helped boost this
vision much closer to the finish line.*

*In addition, I'm indebted to the vision of our Still-
water Strong Memorial Committee. Gary Sparks,
Norman McNickle, John McClenny, Mark Lambert,
Kenny Skillman, Stephen Gose, and Michael Green-
wood each contributed thoughtful ideas, counsel,
and expertise to this effort. The City of Stillwater
designating the property between Main Street and
Hoke Street, along Hall of Fame Avenue as the me-*

morial site, committed key services for construction and future maintenance, serving as a testament to their commitment for this memorial project.

Thank you to every Stillwater Medical employee, first responder, community member, visitor, Oklahoma State alumni, students, faculty, and staff members, who flew into action that day or gave to these projects. Your selfless efforts will be forever remembered by the families to whom it meant most.

To the growing multitude of Stillwater citizens who continue to give and serve, your unselfish acts set us apart from many. A special thank you to her loving volunteers and our passionate Oklahoma State University alumni for inspiring those around you to create, to lead, and to drive future generations of talent, to dream and to do the right thing.

Thank you to all citizens across the state of Oklahoma and to friends stretching from California to Massachusetts; we are eternally grateful for your generosity and for your assistance to our community in a dire time of need. May we forever excel in giving to our fellow man in need and learn from those who succeed, as well as those whom fail.

From behind the scenes, countless others helped in ways no one could ever know. Those are the truly unsung heroes. Those individuals are the ones who quietly and silently invested in sometimes personal and sometimes financial ways that others will never know.

To those unsung heroes, we the Oklahoma State University family, the Stillwater Medical family, the community of Stillwater, the survivors of the 2015 OSU Homecoming catastrophe, and those who lost loved ones that day, say thank you.

The hope, the prayers, and the love you displayed for our friends and our community will forever be remembered. We'll forever thank you for being Stillwater Strong... Loyal and True!

CPSIA information can be obtained
at www.ICGtesting.com
Printed in the USA
FFOW02n0659110518
46395270-48557FF